Change the Way You See Yourself

The Mental Detox Guide to Coping With Depression, Embracing Forgiveness, and Learning to Love Yourself

Kiffany Dugger

Unless otherwise noted, all Scripture verses are taken from the Holy Bible, New International Version. NIV. Copyright @1973,1984,2011 by Biblica, Inc. Used by Permission, All Rights Reserved Worldwide

NIV Thinline Bible
Published by Zondervan
Grand Rapids, Mi 49350

Change the Way You See Yourself: Learn How to Clean out Your Emotional Trashcan to Reclaim Your Authentic Self
Copyright © 2016 Kiffany Dugger
Published by The Bourgeois Group
Houston, TX 77284

All rights reserved. No part of this publication may be reproduced, stored in a retrieval system, or transmitted, in any form or in any means – by electronic, mechanical, photocopying, recording or otherwise – without prior written permission.

ISBN:978-0-692-62950-5
Printed in the United States of America

I dedicate this book to my uncles, Howard Hughes and Edward Archie. Rest in heaven, I love you always.

ACKNOWLEDGMENTS

Much of how we see ourselves, how we treat others, our negative thoughts, insecurities, fears and the way we allow others to treat us is a direct reflection of our inability to see ourselves as God sees us; fearfully and wonderfully made. Changing the way you see yourself is not about new clothes, new hair, new makeup, or augmenting body parts to make yourself look better physically. It's about healing from the inside out. If you don't feel good about who you are at your core, cosmetic enhancements won't amount to a hill of beans; you'll still be a mess wrapped in a beautiful package.

I could not have found the strength to empty my emotional trash can, recycle the remnants of my brokenness into my testimony and share this book with you without fervent prayer and faith God was guiding me every step up the way. I thank God for loving me when I didn't have the strength to love myself. I thank Him for His "Yes" as well as His "No."

I thank my shepherd, Ralph Douglas West for his uncut, theologically sound Biblical teaching; his preaching has fed my hungry soul. When I felt shame and didn't love myself He taught me that nothing can separate me from the love of God. Be who you are authentically and don't care who don't (no typo) like it. I thank my family (Mommy, Aunt Thell, Daddy Carl, Grandma Dolly, Granddaddy Mose and Rodney) for laying the foundation and modeling love, strength, and faith. I thank my cousins Karla and Paige for their unyielding support. I thank Ray Davis for pushing me to complete this book and encouraging me every step of the way. I thank my sister-friends for understanding my true introverted, eccentric personality and supporting me no matter what. I thank Rev. Jewel London for her powerfully anointed prayers and pushing me out of my comfort zone. I thank Jacquie Hood-Martin for reassuring me that who I am, authentically at my core is more than enough. Thank you Dr. Betty Womack for telling me, "yes, you can and you will do it."

As you prepare to change the way you see yourself, I look forward to taking this journey with you.

Contents

Introduction: The Generosity of Emptiness 1

1 The "Self-Seeding" Gardner 5

2 The Bastard from Mississippi 11

3 Searching for an Exit Wound 23

4 Emptying the Overflowing Human Trash Can 31

5 The Common Cure for
the Emotionally Malnourished Woman 41

6 Too Full To Be Blessed 51

7 Leased Without an Option To Buy 61

8 What Will You Do with One String? 67

9 Learning to Limp With Grace 75

10 Unapologetically Authentically Bourgeois 81

Who Am I Authentically? 89

Introduction

The Generosity of Emptiness

Have you ever felt like you were sitting at the bottom of a barrel, weighed down with the burdens of depression, grief, abuse, and unforgiveness? Are you running on empty and feel as though you have nothing left? Are the pages of your life-book stained with the residue of a painful past? If your answer to these questions is yes, you have taken the first step in acknowledging that your emotional trashcan is overflowing and should be emptied immediately.

When we enter the world, we are not given a life map or a blueprint that will chart our exact course. Our parents are not handed a handbook that reveal step-by-step instructions outlining our journey from beginning to end. Every one of us has a story to tell. The contents of our individual life-books may vary from beginning to end, but somewhere in the middle, our pages are stained with residue from our emotional trashcans. Somewhere in between birth and death, reality steps in and dire situations occur at the most inopportune times. Tragedy strikes, unemployment sends us into a financial tailspin, a loved one dies, or domestic violence invades our relationships. These unwelcome circumstances, along with other countless other factors, test our faith, filling our emotional trashcans overflowing them with uncontainable debris.

A few years ago, I found myself sitting right where you are, in the middle of a trash heap trying to sift through the rubble of my brokenness. My physical health began to fail me once again, and I was holding on to my sanity by a split end. I'd reached a point where I felt like I had nothing left. Actually, I felt like I was juggling wet noodles. My life was hard to grasp, and the pieces that I could catch a hold of were breaking apart in the palms of my hands. I'd been unemployed for almost two years, battling depression, trying to build a successful business brand, dodging bill collectors, facing eviction, and literally counting pennies one by one—all while trying to keep up appearances to deflect attention from what a mess I was in.

Finally, God answered my prayer for employment—only for me to hear Him say that the job would not be easy, but necessary to prepare me for His purpose. As a human being, I could not understand what was about to happen in my life. In the midst of yet another desert filled with emptiness, I prayed fervently that the Lord would reveal His plan to me. I couldn't wait for it to be revealed in His time. Instead, I needed to know immediately what the future held. Already in a dry place, I desperately needed God to quench my thirst in the midst of a spiritual drought, and here God was again, telling me to wait. The last thing I wanted to do was wait.

I had reached the bottom of the barrel, so I felt that nothing of any use remained. In fact, all I had left was the trash that I'd collected throughout my life. What could I do with guilt, shame, abuse, unforgiveness, abandonment, and anger? How could I even begin to sift through the clutter and reclaim what was rightfully mine? How could I wait one more second for an answer from God? For months, the answers to these questions escaped me. And then one day, it happened. I was at a conference where I heard someone say, "You never just have nothing." In that moment, I encountered what I like to call "the generosity of emptiness."

I'm sure you're asking, "What is so great about having nothing and being empty? How can something really come from nothing? How can you turn the trash that fills your emotional trash can into recycled treasure?" The answer is simple: God is omnipotent. He is the only one powerful enough to make something out of nothing. You cannot be full unless you are empty. Sometimes, God has to take us, turn our world upside down, shake us, and empty out all the garbage that we've been holding on to—only to fill us up again with His blessings. God had to break me and take away the security of a job, my health, material possessions and all those things that I had put my trust in to call my attention to the fact that I was living in the middle of an emotional trash heap.

My prayer changed from "Lord, I need a job" to "Lord, I need to be whole again. Fix me, Jesus." I asked God to reveal to me those people and things that I needed to rid myself of. I realized that I'd been holding on to trash from over twenty years ago. I was holding on to people who served no purpose in my life but to fill space. Some of my friendships had become exhausting obligations in which I was allowing myself to be leased without an option to buy. I was emotionally drowning in a poisonous sea of unforgiveness. I was overflowing with so much junk that I needed God to empty me to fill me up again. So I asked myself, *How can I dig my way out of depression, hopelessness, and shame in order to see myself as God really sees me?*

To see myself as God sees me, I had to change the way that I saw myself. How did I change the way that I saw myself? How could I clean out the emotional trash that had been festering in my spirit? Well, I'm glad you asked. I had to work hard at it. I had to first admit that I was a hot mess, and then commit to healing myself by confronting my past. At the same time, I had to realize that in order to be filled, I needed to be empty. I also realized that my trash could be recycled in order to help someone else.

My friends and I get together every so often and participate in an activity that we call trash-to-treasure. Each person finds something they no longer use or need and brings it to the home of whomever is hosting the party. Items range from clothing, small appliances, accessories, and other discards that may be of use to someone else. The items are tagged and labeled with numbers. During the course of the game, each person selects a number, allowing him or her the opportunity to choose an unwanted item that someone else has brought. At the end of the night, everyone leaves with something that was of no use to the person that brought it, but had become a blessing to another person.

Through His grace, mercy, and impeccable timing, God has emptied me and filled me up again. Just like the "trash to treasure" game, I no longer need to hold on to the negative experiences of my past. This book outlines my journey from hoarding my trash to purging it and recycling it into my testimony. Writing this book puts my life on display for dissection. With much transparency, I provide an honest account of my life story in which I reveal my fears, vulnerability, and shame. This book is intended to give you a jumpstart as you begin to clean out your emotional clutter.

My prayer has always been that God would bless me to bless someone else. Unfortunately, my expectation of a blessing used to be tied to money. It took me a while to realize that God was preparing my trash to not only bless me, but to encourage someone else as well. Just when I thought I was empty and had nothing left to give, I discovered a whole trashcan full of recyclable clutter. It is almost impossible to imagine how a series of unfortunate events kept me from seeing myself as God sees me and left me feeling like I had nothing left to give. I never dreamed that useless debris from an overflowing emotional trashcan could be considered a blessing. Now I'd like to share this blessing with you, while encouraging you to change the way that you see yourself.

1
The "Self-Seeding" Gardner

On the coldest day of winter, the frigid wind swept across the playground, burning my cheeks. Warm tears streamed down my face, almost freezing in mid-stream. The air was cold, and the Michigan hawk was whipping at what seemed like a speed of a hundred miles an hour. The sound of my voice screaming, "Stop . . . stop . . . please let me go" silenced everything else around me. My teeth felt like icicles, and my body was in excruciating pain as I felt my arms being pulled and my body being pushed through an iron gate. For a brief moment, I'd lost track of what was happening. It seemed like everything happened in an instant. One moment I was on the playground huddling with my friends trying to keep warm, and in the next moment, I was being pushed and pulled through a narrow iron gate. Two of my male classmates were trying to see if I was "skinny" enough to fit through a gate on the playground.

As I screamed, I could hear my friends yelling for them to let me go. The other children looked and laughed in amusement at my pain. As the boys pushed and pulled my body, I could feel the bars pressing against my chest. At that moment, I experienced the worst pain I'd ever felt in my life. Not only was I physically wounded, but I was also embarrassed. I could feel myself dying inside as I heard the kids yelling what I felt were insulting nicknames: "Toothpick," "String Bean," "Beanpole," and just plain old "Skinny." Ironically, in my mind I was wondering if I could actually fit through that gate. I kept saying to myself, *Please don't let me get stuck in this gate.* I could imagine my chest being crushed, pushing the life right out of me. Suddenly, I saw the playground attendant running toward me, and I knew I would be saved. She would make the boys release me so that I could breathe again. The closer the attendant got, the faster my heart beat. By the time she reached me, my body felt hot and heavy.

When she pulled me out, I was crying uncontrollably because my feelings were deeply hurt and I was deeply embarrassed. Some of the other children were still laughing and hurling insults, which felt like venom sinking into my skin and penetrating my soul. As I looked at the faces of the mob of children gathering around me, pointing and laughing, I felt like the loneliest little girl in the world.

On that cold winter day on a snow-covered Michigan playground, I learned a lesson that would stick with me for most of my life. At ten years old, I'd learned to hate myself. I learned that sticks and stones could definitely break my physical bones, but malicious words could do even greater damage: they penetrated my very soul and lived with me for what seemed like an eternity.

You still may not understand how that incident could have affected me the way it did. Some say that I should be happy to be "skinny" versus "fat." The truth is there are thousands of little girls that all over the world right now obsessing over being "fat." Living next door to the little girl who is starving herself because she is being teased for being over weight is a little girl who is stuffing her bra and wearing booty pads because someone has told her that she is too "skinny." When you are told at a young age that you are physically flawed, it is difficult to conceive of any other image than a negative one.

Most people can't understand my insecurities about my weight. Well, let me paint the picture for you to help you realize how I broke into a million little pieces. While I was growing up, other children and even adults would curl their lips in disgust and screw up their faces with looks of revulsion when they saw me. They'd tell me that I needed to eat and often compared me to starving children in Africa. Often people I just met would grab my wrist and form a circle with their index finger and thumb to measure how "skinny" I was. Others would look at me and simply say, "Damn, you skinny!" Men would look at me and say, "You have a pretty face, but you're too skinny," or "Your butt is too flat." To avoid teasing, I started shopping alone because my so-called friends would go shopping with me and constantly comment on how skinny I was, as if it were an abnormality or disease. As I tried on clothes, they would make comments like, "You are too skinny," or "You need to eat."

I was so self-conscious and hated my body so much that I spent hundreds of dollars on products that would help me gain weight. I gorged myself with fast food and ate late at night consuming foods high in calories, just so I would pack on the pounds. This compensatory

1 The "Self-Seeding" Gardner

habit developed into an unhealthy obsession with foods high in saturated fat and calories that I'm still trying to control. I would drive up to a fast food restaurant and order three hamburgers, an order of nuggets, a large fry and a large soft drink. After ordering all that garbage, I'd sit in the car and gorge myself trying to pack on the pounds. I wore clothes that hid my body and wouldn't be caught dead in a pair of shorts or a short skirt. I hated everything about myself. I was constantly thinking of ways to make myself more appealing. I bought tons of weave, makeup, expensive clothes, and fashionable shoes to make myself more physically attractive. On the outside, I looked like I had everything together—that I was stable and knew what direction I was headed. I was "skinny" with high cholesterol and high blood pressure. On the inside, I was a jacked-up mess because at the end of the day when I looked in the mirror, I saw imperfections that I could not erase.

Some time ago, I was recovering from an illness that left me physically and emotionally depleted, which drove me into a deep depression for two years. During my illness, however, I wrote my first novel, entitled *The Green-Eyed Butterfly*, along with two other novels to be released soon. While preparing to release *The Green-Eyed Butterfly*, I searched for the near-perfect model to capture the essence of Seth St. James, the character I'd created. Realizing my funds were low, I feared my vision for the cover would be compromised. My branding is very important to me, and I wanted everything to be just right. This was my first book, and the main character had already become a part of me; she is, in fact, my alter ego.

With no resources to pay for the perfect model, I decided to throw on some green contact lenses and take the picture myself. Posing for my own cover seemed like a ridiculous and desperate attempt to accomplish something I was sure would fail. Deep down in my heart, I wanted to put on pretty clothes, take a beautiful picture, and hope the camera would do its magic by making me beautiful. Being Seth would transform me into someone I wanted to be: confident, sexy, fearless, and beautiful.

After searching for a local photographer, I could not find anyone whom I trusted with my vision, so I felt defeated. But then a friend suggested that I contact a photographer named Mic Fontaine. While planning my photo shoot, I perused Mr. Fontaine's photo gallery and discovered he did amazing work transforming "ordinary" people into extraordinary works of art. Going into the photo shoot, I was extremely apprehensive. In my mind I wasn't nearly beautiful enough to be photographed and plastered all over promotional material, but there was still a glimmer of hope living deep within my soul. My thought process at the time was that Mic and his styling team would transform me into the person I truly wanted to be. I thought they would make me look like someone else, someone who was confident and fabulous.

I remember the exact moment Mic called to tell me to check my e-mail: my proofs were ready. I hung up the phone and sat at my desk, staring at the wall for approximately five minutes. I was bracing myself for the worst. In my mind, because it was me in those pictures, nothing about them would be right. I felt that no matter how much makeup, hair, and new eyes were applied, it was still me—and I was "ugly." Finally, I logged into my account and checked Mic's e-mail. When I downloaded the photo, my mouth flew open, and I was actually stunned. Staring back at me was a beautiful, fabulous, and confident woman, and that woman was me. Mic took a photograph of me that would change the way I saw myself forever. After I saw what he'd created, I was amazed at how beautiful I truly am. Please don't misinterpret this as a statement of conceit. Accept this as the moment I found peace, along with the strength to find that little girl I'd lost decades ago. Of course, Mic worked his magic and added some airbrushing (a fierce makeup artist didn't help), but at the end of the day it was still me. I *did* have what it took to make that photo command attention.

As my business relationship with Mic grew, a true and sincere friendship blossomed. He is not my friend just because his efforts helped me to realize superficial physical beauty. Instead, through his encouragement and love, he led me to rediscover the person that had been lost for so long. Mic once shared with me this awesome concept about how his photography helps to change the way women see themselves. He explained that for one reason or another, people have insecurities that alter their perception of themselves. As a photographer, he encounters many broken women who are unhappy with themselves. He feels that his job is to expose the real essence of a person's beauty, from the inside out.

For me, this restoration of confidence was like watching a wilting flower regaining its bloom. One of my most cherished childhood memories was watching my grandmother work in her flower garden. In her flowerbed, which was the length of the driveway, the flowers she grew were beautiful, exotic, and vibrant. She spent every Saturday planting, pruning, watering, and tending to her prize-winning flowers. Each year I noticed that some of the flowers would bloom like clockwork, while some would die at the end of the season and never return. My grandmother explained to me that the annuals only lasted for a season, but the perennials had longevity, blooming each year and thriving for more than one season.

1 The "Self-Seeding" Gardner

When I got older, I planted a flower garden of my own. Soon I noticed that flowers were growing where they had not been planted. Of course, I went to my most trusted source that never let me down: Google. I discovered that annuals are fair-weather flowers that offer no long-term commitment. They are planted from a seed, and if the wind blows, the annual seeds could fly off to other areas of the garden and plant themselves, causing other annuals to grow in an unplanned spot. This is called "self-seeding." Perennials are the most consistent of the two, even though they are less vibrant in color and their blooms have a shorter lifespan than annuals.

In some aspects, gardening is much like the changing seasons of life. After a seed of insecurity is planted, we water it, feed it, and watch it grow into a plant that is difficult to manage. Some of these emotionally damaging seeds are like self-seeding annuals. We tell ourselves that we are unworthy, ugly, fat, too skinny, and not good enough, so we conclude that nobody loves us. We plant negative seeds, and they continue to spring up in other areas of our lives like our marriage, our job, friendships, church, relationships and parenting.

Although the two boys on the playground planted the negative seeds that made me think something was physically wrong with me, for most of my life, I have been guilty of planting "self-seeding" annuals. No matter how many times people told me that I was attractive, it didn't matter. For every one positive affirmation, five negative insults took root. I let insecurity and doubt fertilize those "self-seeding" annuals and blow them into other areas of my life, planting more challenges where they should not have been.

Gardening can be tedious and more responsibility than some can handle. The time- consuming nature of gardening can cause some to abandon their garden, leaving it overgrown with weeds, wild flowers, and stray branches. As a gardener, there are three important aspects of gardening that I have learned: the success of the plant's growth depends on the type of seed planted, how the seed is fertilized, and the pruning of dead branches.

The good news is that you don't have to depend on your human gardening skills for restoration and fertilization of your self-esteem. God's love is planted in you and restores you when you wither and begin to fade. Whether "self-seeding" annuals or strategically planted perennials are growing branches of doubt, low self-esteem, insecurity, and hopelessness in your life, God can prune and cut away those branches restoring you and changing the way you see yourself!

After reading the "Self-Seeding Gardner," are you able to identify negative seeds that you or someone else has planted in your internal garden? Take an inventory of your internal garden and list negative seeds that have been planted.

Reflect on the scripture below. After reading the scripture and realizing God created you in His image, how do you feel about yourself at this moment?

So God created mankind in his own image, in the image of God he created them; male and female he created them.
Genesis 1:24

Write a prayer thanking God for creating such a wonderful human being (You) in His own image. Ask God to help you rediscover the wonderful person that lives inside you.

2
The Bastard from Mississippi

Growing up, I wasn't completely aware that my biological father was missing from my life. For the first ten years, my household included my grandmother, aunt, grandfather, and our dog Peaches. My mother moved to Detroit when I was three years old, she would visit us during the holidays, and I'd spend the summers with her. My family dynamic wasn't strange to me because quite a few of my friends were being raised by their grandparents. In some cases, parents and grandparents raised children together in the same house. For some children across the globe, being raised in a multi-generational household is still considered normal. In my case, I was a normal kid living with the all-American family. In fact, I had everything in a family that a little girl could need or want. As far as I knew, life was near perfect until someone told me differently.

During a life-altering moment that as an adult I now can excuse as childhood ignorance, I changed the way that I saw myself, along with my value as my parents' daughter. At an age when I should not have been worried about body image, happiness, and fitting in, I added one more issue to my list of worries: I found out that I was a bastard.

The events leading up to the moment when I realized that I was a bastard are a bit fuzzy to me. I can't even remember my exact age at the time. All I remember is that my cousins and I were sitting in my aunt and uncle's living room, doing much of nothing, when my older cousin asked me about my daddy. She asked me why no one had ever seen him. Suddenly, the conversation changed from an innocent, carefree moment between children to a paradox of confused clarity. Up until that moment, I had not given much thought to my parents' union or lack thereof. I called my grandfather "Daddy Carl," and that had been good enough for me. When I was in the first grade, I learned about the normal family structure, which indicated that every family should have a mother and a father; but mine didn't, so I just continued to draw pictures of the people who lived in my house and moved on with my life.

After the million-dollar question about my father was asked, I sat in the middle of the room, feeling like there was a huge, blinding spotlight shining directly in my face. What should I say? I had no idea what to say because I didn't know anything about my father. I had never given him a second thought. Still feeling like I should say something, I looked around at the faces of my cousins waiting with bated breath for me to reveal the mystery of who my father was and why they'd never seen him. No matter how dysfunctional they were, all of the kids in the room had some type of relationship with their fathers, but I was the odd one out. I was the only one in the room who knew absolutely nothing about their father.

Swallowing the lump in my throat, I sat there trying to visualize my father, but I could not muster one single image of him. I couldn't definitively say that I knew anything about him. I began to ask myself: *Who is he? What does he look like? What is his name? Do I look like him? But most important, now that you mention it, where in the hell is he?* My mind raced a thousand miles a minute, trying to find an answer to the question. I began to get frustrated because I had nothing to say, and I felt like I wanted to disappear.

A few moments passed, and I couldn't continue to stall. The answers I was looking for could not be found outside the window that I was staring straight through, while hoping that the subject would soon change. Reluctantly, I looked over and revealed that I had no idea who my father was. As far as I knew, I had never seen him or even heard his voice. Once I admitted to myself and the universe that my father was a mystery to me, I felt deflated, like the wind had been let out of my body. I sat there feeling like something was wrong, but I had no idea what.

Wearing a smirk on her face and emitting a cynical laugh, my cousin said, "You're a bastard." With great pleasure, she continued to tell me that because I was a bastard born out of wedlock, I was a sinner who would go to hell. After the floodgates had been opened, she didn't let up for air. All of her insults were raining down on me like drops of acid. As the word "bastard" continued to fly through her lips, I felt like I wasn't human—like there was something wrong with me. I wanted to disappear or cry out, "Stop it, leave me alone," but I knew that I couldn't show fear. So I just sat there, wishing that she'd choke on that word.

Just when I thought I'd pulled myself together, my cousin told me that I was a mistake and neither of my parents wanted me. In an instant, I felt something click inside me, as if some sort of light switch had been turned on. My family dynamic before moving to Detroit now began to make sense to me. In my mind, I had concluded that my parents didn't want me, so they forced me to live with my grandparents.

While sitting there trying to figure out what had just happened, I couldn't quite identify how I felt, but I knew that something inside me had changed. I felt exposed and violated, as if I'd been robbed of the feeling of being loved and wanted. Up until that point, I felt loved and wanted by my family, but all that had been washed away by one detail: I now realized that I was a bastard.

For the rest of the day, the word "bastard" sat on my chest like a fragile wooden pallet loaded down with bricks. Although I didn't have a true understanding of what the word meant, I was no stranger to it because "bastard" flew out of my grandfather's mouth like he owned the patent on it. I knew that it was an ugly word I was forbidden to use. Upon hearing myself being called a bastard, I knew that whatever it was, I didn't want to be one.

Before I was told that I was a bastard, my immediate family had been my security blanket. I knew for sure that my grandparents, aunt, and mother loved me. For the first time, I was made painfully aware that I wasn't normal, and the possibility that I was an unwanted mistake was heartbreaking.

Loaded with thousands of questions, I waited anxiously for my mother to pick me up from my aunt and uncle's house. My plan was to immediately fire off my questions one by one; but once our eyes met, I could not bring myself to approach the subject.

Fortunately, my grandfather taught me that if I didn't understand what a word meant, I should look it up. Later that night after returning home, I pulled out the dictionary and researched the word "bastard." The word has two different definitions: 1) a person born of parents who were not married; and 2) an unpleasant person. This definition confirmed my worst fears: I was a horrible person because my parents were not married and I had no father whom I could accurately identify. To add insult to injury, I could not forget that my cousin told me I was a sinner on my way to hell. For weeks I thought about how terrible I must be because I was a bastard. I started to wonder if my father had abandoned me because I was born bad.

Going to church has always been a part of my life. In fact, I can never remember a time when I didn't go to church consistently, so I thought I had a pretty good idea of what sin was. I knew that a sinner was something bad. Wanting to know exactly what bastards looked like, what they ate, and where they lived, I finally got up the courage to ask my Sunday School teacher to explain to me exactly what a bastard was. She told me that a bastard was an illegitimate child, but I had no idea what "illegitimate" meant. I asked her to show me the word "bastard" in the Bible, and she opened the Word to Deuteronomy 23:2, which says, "A bastard shall not enter into the congregation of the Lord; even to his tenth generation shall he not enter into the congregation of the Lord." Seeing that I was uncomfortable, my Sunday School teacher realized there was a deeper struggle brewing inside me and I was battling a more serious issue than she could handle. She tried to change the subject, but the damage had been done.

The thought of me being a bastard remained in my mind for it seemed like forever until one Sunday when I was actually paying attention to the sermon, the preacher revealed that God saves sinners. It was like the light bulb had finally come on. No matter how many times I'd heard that God forgives and saves, that day was different. The preacher assured the congregation that even though we are all born into sin, if we confess our sins, then we will be forgiven. It was as if the heavens opened up and a rainbow appeared, with a harp playing in the background. There was hope for my sin-sick soul after all. Before finding out that God does indeed save sinners, I walked around for years thinking that when I died, I was going straight to hell with no possibility of forgiveness.

My problem with being a bastard had been solved, yet there was still a gaping hole in my heart that only my biological father could fill. One question remained in my mind: *Where is my father, and why did he leave me?*

Healing with a Hangover

After I'd gotten over this issue of being a bastard, I began to experience feelings that I could not explain. I noticed that with every phase of my life—childhood, adolescence, college years, and on into full-fledged adulthood—my feelings about being daddyless started to snowball into one big blob of emotional confusion. As time passed, I would allow myself to hurt for just a little while, then I'd tuck the hurt away for a time that was more convenient for me to deal with my emotions. Once a year, I would allow myself to walk around for days in a funky fog thinking about my father's absence and asking myself why he wasn't around, why he didn't support us, and what was wrong with me.

Finally, the pity party had just become too ridiculous and tedious to manage. I had spent so much time and energy on being hurt that I did not focus on healing. One day I was driving down the street and just started yelling, "Lord, I am so tired of this! Help me, please help me!" Frustrated, I pulled into my garage and wearily trudged upstairs. Sitting on the side of the bed, I said, "I'm tired of being angry. Help me please, Lord." After taking a nap in my clothes, shoes, and makeup, I woke up and looked at myself in the mirror. I did not like what I saw. An emotional, out-of-control wreck was staring me in the face. Right then I made the decision that I no longer wanted to heal with a hangover.

If you have ever had the unfortunate opportunity to experience a hangover, then you know that is the physical effect caused by consuming too much alcohol. The night before, you told yourself that you were fine and not intoxicated, but the morning after revealed a different story. In the same way, sometimes we convince ourselves that we've healed and gotten over whatever emotional trauma that we've experienced, until something else comes along, and we experience the hangover of old negative emotions.

I needed to truly heal and not constantly live in a place where I was affected by things that happened over thirty years ago. I couldn't keep drinking the same old nasty, bitter-tasting hate and resentment that I'd been ingesting for most of my life. My first step was discovering the emotion that left me hung over. As He always does in His own mysterious way, God dropped the answer in my lap one Sunday morning while I was sitting in church, feeling unwanted and abandoned, my pastor preached about a group of extraordinary girls called Nakusha.

Abandoning Nakusha

What does it feel like to be unwanted? How does it feel to know that a choice was made by those responsible for your livelihood to brand you as "unwanted"? For decades, in a ritualistic gender selection process, families in Maharashtra, India, named their female children "Nakusha" or "Nakushi" at birth. In the Indian language of Marathi, Nakusha or Nakushi means, "unwanted."

Rejecting the birth of female children, Maharashtra natives believed that sons were better wage earners, promising a more prosperous future for poor families. Having a girl meant that upon marriage, the family would have to pay a dowry to the groom's family. This dowry could prove costly for a family with multiple girls. Naming their female children "Nakusha" would guarantee that the next child born would be a male, creating a greater chance of economic prosperity for the family.

For years, hundreds of girls awoke every morning wearing the brand of "unwanted." Each time they wrote their name, Nakusha, on a homework assignment or were asked to identify themselves by name, these girls were reminded that they were unwanted.

Just a few years ago, thousands of miles across the globe in a country unaware of the emotional trauma caused by this cruel branding of hundreds of innocent little girls, the Nakusha were given a chance to erase the branding of being "unwanted." During October of 2011 in a ceremony sponsored by the Satara district, 280 girls changed the way they saw themselves with a simple change of their name. Some girls picked their own names, while others had names chosen for them by family or friends. Because of this name change, the girls no longer identified themselves as unwanted. A sixteen-year-old girl whose new name is now Sakshi, meaning "witness," revealed her feelings about her new name: "It was symbolic too, since I was going to be a witness to a historic occasion and become part of it too . . . . But now I have a name and I feel good. I feel like a new person. I feel confident. It will change my life forever . . . . Earlier I struggled to give myself an identity. My identity was attached to my family's. Now I feel that I have my own identity."

Even though my parents did not name me Nakusha at birth, the absence of my biological father in my life inadvertently branded me as unwanted, or shall I say that is the way I saw myself. Growing up without my father involved more than just a feeling of being unwanted, but also the mystery surrounding why I was not wanted. My feelings ran deeper than his absence in my life. It involved the unanswered question in my mind, *Why did he choose not to stick around?*

The mystery of being abandoned left me feeling exposed as an unwanted child. In an answer to the question "What is abandonment?" the author of *The Journey from Abandonment to Healing*, Susan Anderson, responds, "Every day there are people who feel as if life itself has left them on a doorstep or thrown them away. Abandonment is about the loss of love itself, that crucial loss of connectedness."

For years I felt as if I had been tossed aside or discarded. I felt disconnected, as if I had lost something. But how could I have felt the loss of something that I never had? The answer is simple: sometimes it is not just the actual loss, but the mystery of the loss. When you have been abandoned, the invisible mystery of the "what if" syndrome kicks in to full gear. Most of my time was spent trying to figure out these questions: Why did he leave? What's wrong with me? Was I not good enough? For many people who have these same questions that go unanswered, their existence continues to be cloaked in a blanket of mystery, leaving them to try and put the missing pieces together.

Like the girls once named Nakusha, God also gives us the opportunity to erase the unwanted branding of abandonment. By His shed blood, Jesus Christ gives us a chance for a new beginning—to wipe the slate clean, erasing remnants of our old identity.

Seeing myself as unwanted and abandoned has cost me more than I can calculate. In my quest to rid myself of the self-inflicted brand of Nakusha, an unwanted little girl holding on to the mystery of abandonment, I realized that I needed to give the little girl living inside me permission to let go and grow up. Letting go meant that I had to forgive, releasing the comfort of anger.

Sometimes we hold on to anger because it is a comfortable emotion. Being angry with someone else and blaming him or her for screwing up our lives takes the pressure off of us for being accountable for our own actions. This means that if we can continue to blame our fathers for not being able to trust, then we don't have to admit that we don't trust because we lack faith that God the Father is our protector. However, faith should not rest in the arms of our earthly father, but God the Father, who has promised to keep and protect us.

Comfortable anger also gives us permission to say, "I am this way because someone did something to hurt me," which misleads us to believe that we can hold others hostage emotionally by constantly reminding them of how their actions hurt us. Wielding this bondage of guilt over people, we force them to try to make amends over and over again. Yet all we really want is an apology or an acknowledgment of wrongdoing from the parent who abandoned us. If all you want to hear is an apology, then apologize to yourself for holding yourself emotionally hostage by letting anger and resentment rule your life.

Give Yourself Permission To Grow Up

If you are reading this chapter and can identify with the pain of feeling abandoned by your father, I wish that I had the magic formula to help you get through the emotional incarceration of abandonment. But my advice is simple: give yourself permission to grow up.

One day I realized the little girl inside me desperately wanted answers and to feel loved and accepted. At the same time, however, the grown woman wanted and needed to realize that having my father in my life was a fantasy. As an adult, when I thought of my father, I mulled over childhood experiences that he missed. I thought about my father teaching me to ride a bike, and later, to drive; sending me off on my first date; taking me off to college; and someday walking me down the aisle at my wedding—all those special things that a daddy does for his little girl. There were plenty of sleepless nights and hazy days spent thinking what it would be like to have my father around. Unfortunately, I didn't realize until I was well into adulthood that, despite my abandonment, I always had everything that a little girl needed. Sometimes we spend more time on the possibility of a "what if" than the tangible certainty of the "here and now."

In my biological father's absence, God blessed me with an amazing grandfather. Daddy Carl, as we affectionately called my grandfather, rarely said a cross word to any of the grandchildren and bragged on us, even to the point of exaggeration. Hearing his voice or seeing his smile was always medicine for whatever ailed me. When I was a little girl, I would sit on pins and needles waiting for my grandfather to return home. If he entered the house twenty times, I would greet him twenty times. Whenever I heard the back door squeak, I'd stop whatever I was doing and rush to meet him with open arms. No matter how many times a day I met him at the door, he would hug me tight and say, "Hey, Sugar." My face would light up, and I'd feel like I'd just won a million bucks.

Almost every night before Daddy Carl went off to close the Laundromat, he'd pick me up and place me on top of his feet and walk me down the hall. As we walked together with my feet on top of his, I would inhale the smell of sawdust and sweat from his hard day's work as a carpenter. I would hold on tight, not worrying about falling because I knew he would catch me if I fell. I knew that I was safe and no one could harm me as long as Daddy Carl was around. With my arms wrapped around his waist, holding on as if my life depended on it, the smell of fresh sawdust danced on the tip of my nose, leaving me lost in a moment that belonged only to my grandfather and me. As days turned into months and months into years, my grandfather continued to walk me on his feet up until a few weeks before he died. The last time Daddy Carl walked me on my feet, I was twenty-four years old, but I felt like I was a little girl again.

2 The Bastard from Mississippi

My grandfather Mose was no different than Daddy Carl. He also loved me unconditionally and made sure that every moment we spent together was special. When he and my grandma Dolly would pick me up for the weekend, he'd drive his vintage black Cadillac sedan. Granddaddy Mose knew that riding in that Cadillac made me feel like royalty and I was his princess. He would escort me to the car, open the door, and help me into the car, and then we'd ride off to the destination of my choice.

Reflecting on those beautiful moments in childhood when the men in my life made me feel safe and special made me realize that as an adult woman, I needed to understand I was letting the needs of the little girl inside me run my life. At that point, I remembered where I am weak God is strong. In His infinite wisdom, God made sure that what my earthly father didn't provide, He provided through the special father figures in my life.

Daddy Carl, Granddaddy Mose, Cousin Harold, Rodney, Uncle Bernard, Cousin Kendall, Cousin Derek, Uncle Creasy, Uncle Howard, and Uncle Brother are among the list of men in my family who intentionally made me feel special, if only for a few moments. While I was growing up, my protectors were my cousins Heath, Tony, Anthony, Avery, and Chris, who would threaten to beat up any man who looked at me the wrong way. My cousin Jun checks on me just because, and my Uncle Claude is one of my biggest supporters. I've been blessed with male friends who showed me the utmost respect and ensured whenever possible, I didn't fall for the okey-doke in relationships. My father did not teach me how to ride a bike, but my cousin Ermon did. My father did not teach me to drive, but Daddy Carl did. My father did not drive me to my first day at Tougaloo College, but my cousin Harold did. My father did not teach me to barbecue, but my uncles Lester and Ed did. My father did not teach me how to fish, but my uncle Bernard did. These men did their best to fill the void left by my biological father's absence.

A girl's relationship with her father is the most important relationship that she will have. He is her first example of how she should be treated. A girl's father sets the expectation bar for every man in her life. The father is the protector, teacher, and provider, as well as an example of how a man treats his family, finances, and friends and honors his commitment to God. Unfortunately today, so many girls grow up without a loving and positive male figure.

People who have been abandoned by their parents are typically unable to form healthy attachments in relationships for fear of being left by a loved one. Each time a relationship fails, it rips the tattered bandage off old wounds left by Daddy years ago. Fatherless girls often grow up to be bitter women who continue to try to fill the void of a missing father. Maintaining a relationship is difficult because there is a lack of trust, the need to feel wanted, or fear of being abandoned all over again. Either these women build a wall to keep men away or they don't have any walls at all, which allows the wrong man to come in and stay until there is nothing left for the right man.

One important thing to remember is that you cannot expect your husband, boyfriend, fiancé, or significant other to fill the void of your father's absence, that isn't his role as the man in your life. The roles are clearly defined: your father is your father, and your husband, boyfriend, man or whatever you call him is just that. So, do not confuse the roles. Theoretically, a father is the one who should protect, teach, and encourage his child, as well as the one who does his best to equip him or her to be a good, upstanding, productive contributor to society.

The simple truth is that anatomy alone does not qualify a man to be a good father. I realized that maybe my father was not ready for the responsibility of fatherhood. Just because a man is able to lie down, stand up, or however a child is conceived, does not mean that he is capable of being a father. Most of the time there are signs that men are not ready to be fathers: he tells you that he does not want children, he has multiple children whom he does not care for in any way, and he is irresponsible in every area of his life. Also, if he is not interested in being with you without a child, there is a strong possibility that a child will not make him stay.

I am grateful I have entered into a healthy space that allows me to see things as they are and not how they should have been. Arriving at this space took quite a bit longer than I'd like to admit. There were some moments in my life when I thought I would never get over my father's absence. The pain of abandonment was so deep; I'd resolved there would always be a gaping hole in my heart that would never be filled. By God's grace, the hole was filled with faith in God, love for myself, and forgiveness.

One morning after sitting up all night trying to figure out how to crawl out of an endless pit of sadness, I realized that throughout my entire life, I have been loved immensely by my family and authentic, ride-or-die friends who knew me, genuinely loved me, and accepted me for who I am. My mother has dedicated her life and sacrificed beyond measure for me to have everything I need and want. My grandparents and aunt made sure that I felt loved, and they protected me and gave me a strong foundation built on Christian values. When I began to weigh the things that I missed from my biological father side-by-side with the things that my Heavenly Father provided, the two really didn't add up.

It is a great possibility that my father and I will never have the relationship that I once longed for, and that is perfectly fine. I am no longer angry and bitter, or sad and discouraged. I no longer feel discarded and empty. I no longer feel exposed; instead, I feel redeemed.

Recommended Reading

West, Ralph Douglas. Left Alone: Finding Strength for Life's Mysteries, Impossibilities and Uncertainties. Houston: Ralph Douglas West, 2008. Print.

Anderson, Susan. The Journey from Abandonment to Healing. New York: Berkley, 2000. Print.

Seamands, David A. Healing for Damaged Emotions. Wheaton, IL: Victor, 1981. Print.

Meyer, Joyce. Beauty for Ashes: Receiving Emotional Healing. New York: Warner Faith, 2003. Print.

Challenge: Write a Letter to Your Younger Self

We are often reluctant to admit we've waisted too much time and energy holding on to the past instead of healing. Writing has always been my way of expressing feelings that I might not otherwise utter aloud. Over time, I have developed the cathartic habit of writing open and honest letters to myself. This practice allows me track my growth as well as identify areas that I need to focus on improving. Ink is a permanent reminder of how I honestly feel about myself, other people and certain situations.

On the following page, I have penned a letter to my twelve year-old self. Based on what you know now, I encourage you to write a letter to your younger self. What advice would you give yourself as a child who feels you're not enough?

Dear Younger Self,

I've spent most of the day trying to figure out the right words to say. I've scribbled over words, erased holes in my paper and stared into space for over an hour attempting to create a profound message to you, my younger self. After careful deliberation, this is what I've come up with; you're blowing it.

You are wasting too much time trying to figure out the why, the how and the why- nots of your life. You're pointlessly spending your days and nights wondering why you're not worthy, why you're not good enough and why you've been left feeling abandoned. Stop worrying about it; your father will never give you an answer that you will accept. Spend less time blaming him and more time understanding that on some level it's really not about you. Unfortunately, not all parents are emotionally equipped to raise another human being. The simple truth is, life is not easy. You can't control the actions of others; you can only control how you respond.

I encourage you to rely less on the love and acceptance of others and more on God's love for you. Stop trying to fit in; don't force relationships of any kind. There will be countless times when you will try and fill the empty space in your heart with people who just don't fit. Don't view this as a form of rejection, but as God's protection. You are a square peg; you're not made to fit in any old hole. Your longing to be accepted and belong to something or someone will only delay God's plan for you.

Life is hard; you will fail at some things and succeed at others. Right now you want to give up; you feel like you're not enough. Just hold on; One day you will read Psalm 139:14 and realize that you do not wear the brand of "Bastard", you wear the banner of one who is "worthy." Love, trust and happiness are not your enemies; not everyone you love will leave you. Your arms are too short to box with God and too frail to shield the world from the mask that you wear, so stop trying to be hard and surrender. Let go and enjoy this wonderful journey called life.

Love,
Your Older Self

3
Searching for an Exit Wound

Unforgiveness is like a traveling bullet, it destroys everything in its path. The unwillingness to forgive is what hinders us from enjoying a healthy and fulfilling life. Harboring resentment, pain, and hatred toward someone who has hurt you emotionally or physically can cause damage that could take a lifetime to repair.

While watching one of my favorite shows, "CSI," I became intrigued by the power of a bullet. In this episode, the CSI team was reviewing the details of how a victim was shot. The CSI team discussed how the bullet had traveled through the body, destroying vital tissue and organs, but there was no exit wound.

At the time I viewed this particular episode, I was in the middle of writing my next novel. Since one of my story characters had been shot, this episode prompted me to research ballistics and the effects of a bullet on the human body. My research revealed that the effect of a bullet on the human body is called "wound ballistics."

In an article entitled "Where's the Best Place To Take a Bullet If You Get Shot?" Josh Clark explains the science behind wound ballistics and the effects a bullet has on the human body when a person is shot. The injury inflicted by a bullet is directly related to the bullet's kinetic energy. Kinetic energy is measured by the bullet's weight, velocity, and gravitational trajectory. The combination of these three factors determines how much damage a bullet will cause to the body.

When a person is shot and the bullet enters the body, it causes an entry wound. Once inside the body, the bullet penetrates bone, tissue, and vital organs. According to Clark, after the bullet enters the body, it passes through tissue, creating a cavity thirty times wider than the path of the bullet. This cavity closes less than a second after the bullet passes through. Once a bullet is sealed in the cavity and travels to make its way out of the body, it can destroy other organs, tissue, and bone, creating shock waves through the body. As the bullet travels through the body, it typically changes direction, causing damage to other areas. The amount of injury the body endures is determined by what the bullet encounters while traveling through the body.

What the bullet encounters also depends on the position of the bullet. There is no exact direction or pattern that a bullet follows; it can be tricky and change positions as it travels. The rate at which the bullet changes its position is called velocity. Average velocity can be defined as the displacement divided by the time. Speed plays a key role in determining damage as well. The average speed of an object is defined as the distance traveled divided by the time elapsed.

Like a bullet traveling through the body, unforgiveness can be deadly. Once the spirit of unforgiveness enters the body, it is sucked up into our emotional cavity and travels through our body, changing direction over the years. This change in direction typically happens at a slow rate, creating shockwaves affecting our physical and emotional health, destroying our families, and suffocating our hopes and dreams. Clark explains that a bullet which stays in the body will generally cause more damage than one that passes through an exit wound because it transfers all of its kinetic energy, ensuring maximum damage.

Harboring hatred and unforgiveness is like retaining a heavy, loaded, slow-moving bullet in your body. Unforgiveness is both an emotional and physical burden. It is almost impossible to heal while holding on to resentment and bitterness. I know you're thinking that it is much easier to say the word "forgiveness" than to actually take action and forgive the one who hurt you, and you are correct. Forgiveness is not an easy task, so preparing yourself to forgive can be an exhausting experience that will push you to your limits. Yet forgiveness is necessary for you to heal.

When I was a child, I experienced sexual abuse that would take me most of my life to work through and overcome. I was not abused by my parents, nor did my family have any knowledge of the abuse while it occurred. My abuser was someone I will call "Victim." You will find out later why I refer to my abuser as Victim.

I was an adult before I verbally admitted to anyone what I'd experienced. It wasn't until I was sitting in my office, reading the file of a child on my caseload who had been abused, that I realized how I had tucked away my own abuse in my emotional trashcan. While wading through the case file, I started to have flashbacks of what happened to me. I didn't realize the depth of my emotional pain until I looked down and saw small puddles of water on my desk that formed from the stream of tears rolling down my cheeks. I touched my wet face and immediately knew I was in trouble. For the next few years, I would be consumed daily with thoughts of what had occurred to me during my childhood. At the time, I was experiencing challenges with my health, so the memories could not have come at a more inopportune time.

I would wake up every morning and convince myself that I could not afford to emotionally break down because my job was to help those forty-two broken children who were depending on me to make them feel safe. The more I tried to convince myself that the abuse inflicted upon me was just a nightmare and nothing really happened, the more I remembered and understood that my experience was very real. The memories were too much for me to handle. I kept trying to forget and move forward, but the shame made me feel exposed, like I was wearing a T-shirt that read, "Damaged Goods." I tried to figure out what role I played in the abuse, but when it all began, I was just a child; so I had no idea what was happening. I didn't understand why I had been chosen, why Victim was so mean to me, and why victim hated me so.

One day, while standing on the balcony of my third-floor apartment, I looked up toward the sky and realized that I needed to get these memories out of my head. I was tired of not sleeping at night and sitting up, staring into thin air like a space cadet. The bad memories had taken over my life, and I could no longer cope with the images that would not stop scrolling through my mind. I thought that if I jumped off the balcony, I would no longer have to live through the memories of what happened. Just as quickly as that awful thought entered my mind, I shook the urge to hurl myself off the balcony out of my head and quickly ran back into my apartment.

I stood in the middle of my living room, shaking. The thought scared the hell out of me. My heart started racing, and beads of sweat started crowning my head. After walking into the bathroom, I washed my face with cold water and stared into the mirror for approximately thirty minutes, trying to figure out how I'd gotten to that point. Although I was a professional social worker who spent my days counseling children about their issues and trying to convince them they would be okay, I could not even properly care for my own emotional needs.

Still standing in front of the mirror, I closed my eyes and took a deep breath. Opening my eyes, I stared into the mirror and asked God to help me get through this terrible time in my life. I did not ask God to help me forget, because I know there are some things that happen in our lives which we will never forget. Nevertheless, with the emotional and spiritual healing Christ provides, we can move past our worst memories with a sound mind and a forgiving heart.

As time passed, I continued to grow in Christ and prayed without ceasing that God would help me through and still allow me to maintain my sanity. During my time of fervent prayer, God worked in His own impeccable timing to reveal to me that my inability to forgive was causing me to be physically and emotionally ill. God also revealed to me five things that would help me see myself not as a bitter, ashamed victim, but someone who is strong, faithful, and triumphant.

1. **Lean not on my own understanding.** My need to work through my issues and not lose my mind in the process had brought me into a closer relationship with God. I was spending more time trying to sift through the years of abuse. Even though I tried to understand how and why I'd been chosen as a victim, I never received the answers that I was looking for. Finally, I realized that I ought not to lean on my own understanding, but instead seek God to help me understand and see what I could not. The hatred that lived in my heart, along with my inability to forgive, was like a bullet that kept changing positions, hitting other vital areas in my life. Somehow I just knew that no matter what type of professional help was available, I still could not make it through without God, who often uses tragedy and trauma to bring us closer to Him. At those moments when I felt like I was alone and no one understood what I was going through, God was closer to me than ever.

2. **There is a blessing in every storm.** My prayer has always been that the Lord would bless me so that I could bless others. Sadly, my expectation of a blessing was always tied to money or material things. Through the process of sifting through my own emotional trash and finding remnants of unforgiveness, however, I realized that I could bless others through my own testimony. As hard as it was and still is to accept, the pain I suffered can bring someone else comfort. It is important for readers to see me not as a victim of one emotionally crippling challenge after another, but as a survivor who is now able to dance in the rain instead of running from the thunderstorms of life.

3. **Hurt People Hurt Other People; Victim was also a Victim.** This step would be the most difficult. One day I was trying to sift through the abuse and the reasons why this happened to me. Only in a moment clearly ordered by God did I realize that Victim had actually been a victim himself. There's one thing you must always remember: you cannot put God in a box. You can't dictate when God will move in your life, and you can't put limits on what He does and how He does it. God can speak into your life in the middle of the night. He can speak in the middle of the desert, or He can speak quietly in the middle of a room full of people.

   God spoke to me while I was driving down the highway, on the way to meet my friends for happy hour. I was recalling a time when I heard Victim's parents tell victim that they wished they had never been born and hoped victim would die. While reliving that exchange between Victim and victim's parents, I could not believe that I was actually beginning to see Victim as a real victim. For the next few days I would think of Victim incessantly and remember the emotionally damaging things I witnessed that happened earlier in victim's life. Somehow, I was able to sift through the debris of my own life and realize that Victim had been abused too. This revelation did not change the fact that what happened to me was wrong and an unnecessary, malicious act, but I was now able to move closer to forgiveness because I now saw Victim as an actual victim.

4. **It's not about me.** One Sunday, I was sitting in church, preparing to take Communion. The choir was singing a song by Donnie McClurkin called "Just For Me." The lyrics to the song are, *"Well, the Cross will always represent the love God had for me/When the Lord of glory, Heaven sent gave all on Calvary/Just for me, just for me; Jesus came and did it just for me."* Sitting in the sanctuary, surrounded by the Holy Spirit and inhaling the fragrance of God's presence, I could not help but picture Jesus nailed to the cross, suffering and dying for my sins. I thought about how Jesus had been sent to earth by God the Father, only to die to save me from my sins. Even though Jesus was sent by God, He still went through unspeakable acts of hatred and abuse while He was here on earth. In the same way, I am not exempt from abuse of any kind. I thought about that moment when Jesus was stretched out on the cross with nails in His hands and a crown of thorns on His head.

While experiencing excruciating pain, He uttered words of forgiveness: "Father, forgive them, for they know not what they do" (Luke 23:34).

One day I'd had more than I could endure, but I still refused to break. I can remember like it happened just a moment ago. Victim chased me around the house, caught me, pinned my arms and legs down, and then spit in my face. Growing up, I was taught that spitting on someone was like saying, "F__ you. You ain't worth nothin." That day, lying on the floor pinned under the oppression of Victim's abuse, something inside me changed my spirit. I decided that I would no longer see myself as a weak victim, but as a hard shell that could not be cracked. I became rigid and mean and vowed that I would never allow any person to emotionally or physically abuse me again.

That was the last day that Victim ever touched me. From that day on, I fought until I was tired. I made up my mind that Victim or anyone else would never hurt me again. As vile and nasty as it sounds, that spit on my face was like a bullet penetrating my body. The poisonous bullet of hatred and unforgiveness had entered my soul, and there was no exit wound. That poison would travel through my body for over two decades, affecting other areas of my life while searching for an exit wound. The only way that wound would truly heal was through forgiveness. When I sat in church and uttered the words of forgiveness, it created an exit wound for all the other garbage to travel through and begin to make its way out.

For me, forgiving my abuser was a long and daunting process. There were moments when hating Victim felt so good that I wanted to hold on to that feeling and never let it go. After confessing my sin of unforgiveness in the sanctuary that day, I knew that some work still had to be done. As you will discover, one of my strengths involves breaking everything down and analyzing it to the lowest common dominator. As a trained investigator and writer, this process comes naturally to me. It has also helped me tremendously through the process of changing not only the way that I see myself, but the way I see things in general. Even though I had forgiven Victim, there were still some moments when I thought about what happened. I decided that I needed to get every detail out in the open, but who could I tell?

My all-time favorite movie is *The Color Purple*. In one scene, after Celie gives birth to her stepfather's baby and he takes the baby from her, he warns her, "You better not never tell nobody but God." One day, while remembering this particular scene, I walked over to my desk and pulled out my "Letters to God" journal and wrote God a letter, confessing my brokenness and my need to heal. I not only mentioned Victim by name in my letters, but I included others I needed to forgive as well. Writing my letter to God revealed two things to me:

1. **I was being supported by a crutch.** One issue that twisted and bound me up in knots was my stubborn refusal deep down in my heart to let go of the hatred. What happened to me was *my* story, so it belonged exclusively to me. The longer I held on to my truth, the longer I could use it as an excuse for my own behavior. Instead of taking responsibility for some of the poor decisions that I made earlier in life, my abuse had become a crutch for explaining why my life was screwed up. I'd let what happened to me rule my behavior and dictate how I would handle relationships with others.

2. **Confession is good for the soul.** Writing down the names of people I needed to forgive (including mine), along with the reasons I needed to forgive them, gave power to my truth. When I finally opened my eyes to see my own brokenness in front of me, I could no longer deny that the elephant was in the room. I would have to hop on that elephant and ride it out of my life. Writing my letter to God helped me not only confess to Him, but also release through the exit wound of forgiveness those bullets that were tearing me up inside.

You might see yourself somewhere in the content of the pages in this chapter. You have been blaming something that happened to you twenty years ago for how you've handled yourself and others throughout your life. It is time for you to realize that holding on to the past has caused you to give up your power. You have been drained of the power of joy, peace, and love because you cannot let go of bitterness. Now, you may be saying, "But you don't know what I've been through." You are absolutely right. I don't know your story, but maybe my experience will help you. The person who hurt you has moved on and is living his/her own life without a care in the world. This individual is married with children, has a great job, lives in a beautiful home, and can sleep at night because he is living on the power that you gave up.

I'm sure that you have been reading this chapter thinking that unforgiveness is not a real word, and to some degree you are correct. While preparing to write this chapter, I needed a clear definition of unforgiveness. I searched for a plausible definition, but I came up empty. It seems that there is no clear definition of the word "unforgiveness" in existence. This alone suggests that unforgiveness does not exist, meaning that we are designed by God to forgive. When you mull over the issue of forgiveness, don't think of yourself or the person who wronged you. Instead, think of Christ and how He has forgiven you for the unspeakable acts that you yourself have done.

4
Emptying the Overflowing Human Trash Can

If you know anything about me, you understand that I love anything that reminds me of Mississippi. For instance, I think the only way to truly appreciate the taste of sweet iced tea is by drinking it from a Mason jar. One day while putting a jar in the cupboard, I accidently dropped it on the floor. The glass was shattered in many pieces and could not be repaired. Reaching down to gather the shards of glass, I noticed that some of the pieces were smaller than others. I was amazed by how many different shapes and sizes of glass had collected on the kitchen floor. The impact of the fall caused pieces of broken glass to scatter everywhere, even to places I never expected.

At that moment, I realized that the amount of damage done to the jar depends on how it was dropped and the impact that was made when it hit the floor. The glass had fallen from my hand, hit the cabinet, bounced onto the edge of the counter, flipping a few times in the air and finally landed on the floor. Before the glass hit the floor, it had taken a journey that allowed it to be chipped at every traumatic impact point.

After the glass broke, naturally I picked up the larger pieces and put them in a plastic bag. I swept the remaining smaller pieces into the dustpan and placed them in a separate bag. Then I carried both bags outside to the recycling bin to be thrown out with the rest of the discarded glass and plastic. I'd spent a great deal of time and energy making sure there was no broken glass left for me to step on and injure myself in the future. As I walked back into the house, I was thinking about how one glass could cause so much trouble.

I realized that the probability of the glass being dropped and ruined for further use depended on how I'd handled the glass in the beginning. In a rush to clean the kitchen and get on with my day, I haphazardly handled the glass roughly, failing to take the time and care I should have to ensure the glass remained secure in my hands and intact for further use. For the rest of the day, I felt disappointment about the way my favorite glass had been broken. Sometimes the way something is broken can have a greater effect on a person than the actual loss of the item. Indeed, the way we are handled can determine the degree of injury upon impact.

Sometimes we handle ourselves as roughly as I handled that glass. We allow ourselves to be dropped, shaken, and bruised; and with each traumatic event, a piece of us is chipped away, leaving us more broken. Yet it is not always other people who cause us injury or harm; sometimes it is our own actions that affect us. Instead of going through the process of healing and purging our emotional debris, we hold on and add other toxic things to an already full emotional trashcan. As we continue to add problems on top of situations and situations on top of issues, we discover that we have turned ourselves into human trashcans.

One of the most daunting housekeeping tasks is taking out the trash. No one wants to do it; but if trash continues to accumulate, it will become rancid and smell up the entire house, making it so unbearable that you are forced to get up and take it outside. Just as you don't want to sit in your home and smell trash, you shouldn't want to carry emotional trash inside your body either, because it will make you so sick that you can't even stand to be around yourself. This emotional collection of debris in the form of hopelessness, abandonment, broken hearts, broken relationships, and past failure can cause you to see yourself as something broken or discarded. In order to take that step toward changing the way you see yourself, you must take an internal inventory and empty out your emotional trashcan.

That day, I chose to throw my broken glass into the recycling bin instead of the trash receptacle because the glass can be recycled into something productive and useful. In the same way, our past experiences should make us stronger, allowing us to turn a negative situation into something positive.

I come from a family that boasts of having thick skin. For most of my professional career, I have had to portray an image of stability to cope with my work environment and not get swept up by the emotionally rough current. For eleven years I worked in the Social Services field, encountering children who were neglected, as well as physically and sexually abused. During my career, I sat in the same room with predators, pedophiles, criminals, and drug addicts. I have encountered children who sexually abused other children, and mothers who gave their children to drug dealers as a form of payment to support their habit. I have sat alone behind closed doors with criminally psychotic people who expressed their desire to skin me alive because they were having visual hallucinations of me as the Devil. I had to maintain my composure and show no fear while trying to help someone who wanted to hurt me.

Through it all, I would sit day after day and listen to other people's issues, trying to help them and make them whole. I wept for the child who had been abused, and my heart broke for the grown man's world that had been destroyed by his mental illness. I watched as young girls continued the cycle of abuse and promiscuity because they had been dropped and broken long ago. I watched my clients suffering from AIDS and often wept because they had no hope. Even though my job was to be objective, it also involved caring for hurting people—but not to the point that I let my emotions render me ineffective.

While I was busy helping others, I ignored my own brokenness and pressed forward in the name of saving the world. I convinced myself that my problems were not half as bad as my clients', so I stored every hurt I experienced in my own personal trash receptacle. Unfortunately, I tucked away so much emotional trash that it started to overflow and spill into my everyday life. My whole personality changed, and I became withdrawn because I had no idea how to deal with all the stuff I had trapped inside my brain. Because I didn't deal with these issues head on, but rather tried to be strong and not show any weakness, I started to break down, piece-by-piece, until one day everything fell apart.

Autumn is always a difficult time of year for me. In the fall of 1999, my grandfather suffered a stroke and died. I stood at the foot of his hospital bed and watched him take his last breath. From that moment on, I was never quite the same. It was like the wind had been knocked out of me. My grandfather meant the world to me because he was the only father I'd ever really known. His death left a hole in my heart so big you could drive a truck through it. There are no words to can describe how much I loved him. To me, he was my daddy.

A month after my grandfather died, my friend Teddy was killed by his roommate. I'm not sure about the particulars of the case, so I won't go into detail. I do know my friend was stabbed to death, and the assailant got away without a scratch. The man accused of the crime served fifteen years in prison and has since been paroled. When Teddy's sister called to tell me the accuser was up for parole, I was sure his parole would be denied. However, he was released from prison and has begun a new life. The man who killed Teddy is living, breathing, eating, working and even has a Facebook page.

Since college, I'd called Teddy my little brother, and he knew I was his "ride or die" friend. Teddy was the first person I called after I learned of my grandfather's stroke. The summer before Teddy died, we spent a week in New Orleans partying like rock stars—without a care in the world.

Two days before Teddy died, he called me, but I did not answer the phone. He left a voice message for me to call him back, but I failed to return his call. When I received the call that Teddy had been killed, I felt like I'd been kicked in the stomach. I had already been crying myself to sleep at night mourning the death of my grandfather, so Teddy's death sent me into overload. I cried for days leading up to his funeral, and then I cried so hard during the funeral, I became physically ill. I lost my voice for weeks, my hair started falling out, and my thyroid condition kicked into overdrive, leaving me physically depleted.

Every day, I would cry for Teddy and my grandfather. I would sit on the floor in the closet or in my car with the radio blasting, lock myself in the bathroom crying, or stand underneath the shower to drown out the sound of my tears. I was in so much emotional pain that I figured I had to be overreacting. A year passed, and I decided enough was enough because it just didn't take all of that. I tucked away my grief, and every time I thought about it, I would just suck it up and move on.

The anniversary of the deaths of both Teddy and my grandfather, coupled with the news that Teddy's murderer had been paroled, added to the emotional trash I'd already been accumulating. At the time, I was already undergoing major personal transitions. I had started working full time after basically having no income for almost two years. Also, I was just getting over a traumatic illness that left me bedridden for months. As I was trying to adjust to challenges on my new job, I found out someone I trusted was really stabbing me in my back. I was in a relationship I should have never been in. My books were not selling, and my thyroid condition was yet again out of control. I had so much emotional crap bottled up inside that I was convinced I was finally losing my mind. To top it all off, God revealed His plan for my life, but it had nothing to do with the plans I had.

Withdrawn and depressed, I had no interest in interacting with anyone. All I wanted to do was sit at home and write or lie in my bed. I had become a basket case, with no control over my emotions I was crying all the time. I couldn't stay focused and I stopped caring about most things.

When Teddy's sister told me his murderer was up for parole, it was like picking a scab off an old wound. For weeks, I was glued to my computer, searching for news and information on Teddy's murder because I wanted to know details I had refused to hear years ago. I researched material about Teddy's attacker and found his inmate information. Every day, I logged on to my computer and stared at the face of the man who was responsible for taking my friend's life. Finally the day had come: I found out Teddy's murderer had been paroled on a Monday.

For the next two weeks, I walked around like a fragile piece of glass. If you looked at me wrong, I cried. While sitting at my desk at work, I desperately tried not to break emotionally. I made it until Saturday night at 11:13 p.m., when I got out of bed. After walking to the garage and retrieving a bucket of hot-pink paint I had purchased the week before, I removed everything from my office and placed it in the hallway. Then I lined the floor with drop cloths and plastic, removed the electrical and light covers, and taped up the baseboards. I opened the paint can, stirred the paint, poured it into the pan, put the roller on the end of the rolling stick, and started painting my office walls pink at midnight.

As the walls changed from antique white to fuchsia, I spread the paint up and down the wall. With each stroke of the roller, tears began to fall from the corners of my eyes. At first I wept silently, and then I opened my mouth and started to bawl like an injured child. I could feel something brewing inside me that was about to erupt like a volcano. With the roller still in my hand, I fell to the floor with my back pressed against the wet paint, and I cried like a wounded animal until I saw daylight.

I cried for things I'd blocked out that happened to me as a child. I mourned the death of my relationship with my father. I cried because I had been angry with my mother for over a decade because it took us so long to arrive in Mississippi after my grandfather had his stroke that I did not have the chance to say good-bye. I cried because I did not return Teddy's call. I cried because the man responsible for his death was breathing while Teddy was not. I cried because four siblings I'd placed in New York in an adoptive placement years ago had been separated, so I felt like I failed them. I cried because I was late getting to the hospital before my aunt Pauline died the year after my grandfather and Teddy passed. I cried because for years I was unable to get the image of watching my grandfather lying in a hospital bed and taking his last breath out of my head. I cried because in 2009 following surgery to have a 9-cm (the size of a full-term baby's head) fibroid tumor removed from my uterus, I almost died from an infection that started to spread through my body, leaving me with an open wound that I had to clean every single day, twice a day for six months until my incision finally healed.

If that paragraph just made your head spin, then imagine how I felt. There is a list a mile long of issues I confronted that night. It was as if I was that child on the playground all over again, being pulled through iron bars. I had been stretched as far as I could, so I could go absolutely no further in the condition I was in. After sitting on the floor and crying into the early morning, I felt like a ton had been lifted off my chest. I was still weighted down because that was just the beginning of my healing process, but instead of continuing to fill my emotional trash can with all the garbage I'd accumulated over my lifetime, I began designing a plan to dig my way through and see myself as God's treasure and not discarded trash.

My first step was prayer. After asking the Lord to cleanse me and make me whole, I begged Him to forgive me for poisoning my body with all that emotional trash and not trusting in Him. I knew it was possible for a therapist to help me, but it was a reality that the Lord would indeed bring me through. I spent hours in my closet, sitting on a pillow in complete darkness and silence, listening to that still, quiet voice speak to me in the way only God can.

Writing has always been cathartic for me and has served as a safe escape, so I started journaling. I wrote down my feelings about everything I could think of. Soon, however, my journaling took a different turn. I started writing letters to God and placing them in small envelopes I still keep in a wooden box that belonged to my grandfather. My letters to God were filled with intimate thoughts I could not share with anyone but Him. I realized how much I needed to get some of the trash swimming around in my head on paper where I could see it. Even though I needed to tell someone my innermost secret thoughts, feelings, and fears, there was no one in the world I could trust with my trash but God.

I had acknowledged my issues and confessed them, but now that I was confronting all of this crap bottled up inside my body, what was I going to do with it? Was I just going to pat myself on the back and say, "Way to go, you got all that out"? Nope, I had to do something. I was sitting in the middle of a big pile of crap that I'd pulled from every secret place in my life and it stank, so now what?

Getting rid of emotional trash is a process. It took me years to collect all of the emotional, physical, and mental garbage that had me weighed down, so I knew the healing would not be a quick fix. I had to put in some work, so I treated myself just like I was one of the fiction novels I'd been working on. On paper, I created a project management outline that included an action plan and a communication plan, as well as the goals and objects for my journey. I wanted to put as much time and effort into discovering the real me as I did the characters that do not exist. I made a list of items I would need, which consisted of the following:

- 3 corkboards
- 3 index cards of different colors (4x6)
- Push pins
- Sharpies
- Tape
- A picture of myself when I was happy
- A new journal
- Ink pens/pencils
- Post-it Big Pads

After collecting all these items, I hung the corkboards on the walls in my office. Above the top board, I taped two pictures I found of myself taken during a time in my life when I was happy and felt whole. My smile was beautiful and bright. I just knew this happy version of me was somewhere inside, waiting to get out. Next, I wrote, *"Purging my Emotional Trashcan"* on a large Post-it pad and taped it next to the picture.

After naming my board, I completed the 4x6 pink, brown (the color of a paper bag), and beige cards. (My choice of colors wasn't all that significant; they were just colors I liked at the time.) On the pink cards I wrote down the names of the different kinds of trash I needed to clean from my life and pinned them across the top of the corkboard. On the beige cards, I wrote my specific challenge, and on the brown cards I wrote my action plan. For every issue, I created a solution and action items. I gave myself a realistic timeline (which included short-term and long-term goals) for progressing in those areas.

- Example:
  - **Pink Card**: emotional and psychological factors that keep me down
  - **Beige Challenge Card**: social anxiety
  - **Brown Action Card**: Commit to attending one social outing a month for three months. Whether it was eating dinner with a friend, attending a party, or even getting fully dressed and going to the mall to window-shop, I was going to release myself from the bed and my walls at home.
    - When I returned from my outing, I wrote down how I felt— In increments of thirty days, I would document my progress or things I needed to focus more attention on.

Some of the trash listed on my pink cards included the following issues: 1) how I would stop procrastinating and maintain consistency in my everyday life; 2) names of people I need to grant limited access to; and 3) how I would free myself from debt and save more money.

This may seem a bit much for some, but I am visually oriented. It was important for me to see my issues in front of me, and I needed to see my progress as well. The journals and board gave me a specific system to chart my progress or any setbacks. I was able to see what activities worked for me, what my triggers were, and ways to stay motivated.

During this process, I learned to be grateful for the trash that filled my emotional trashcan. Sometimes God can use our trash as a testimony to bless someone else. My prayer has always been that God would bless me so I could be a blessing to someone else. God gathers our broken pieces and uses His grace, mercy, and the gift of a second chance as the glue that will mend us and make us whole again!

4 Emptying the Overflowing Human Trash Can

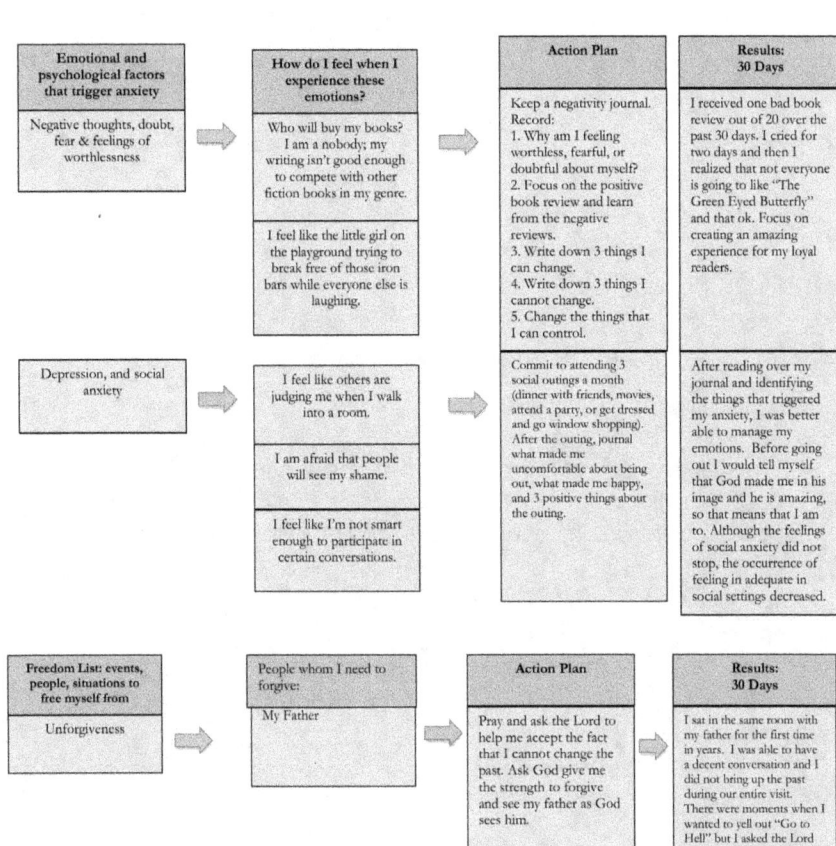

Sometimes we are buried beneath the debris that fill our emotional trashcan; we are unable to see our true selves, but God knows who we are authentically. Read and reflect on Psalm 139. After reading and meditating on Psalm 139, what areas in your life would you like to focus on healing?

1.

2.

3.

4.

5.

What fears do you have about identifying the items that fill your emotional trashcan? How does Psalm 139 minister to you as you prepare to empty your emotional trashcan?

Prayer Lord, I desire to see myself as you see me. I confess, I am weighed down with the burdens of remembering a painful past, unforgiveness, fear and feelings of an uncertain future. Somewhere along the way I became lost, but I know only you can help me find my way. Search me oh Lord, reveal those areas in my life that need healing. Lord, continue to be a hedge of protection around me as I seek to purge myself of those things that serve as a distraction. Lord, order my steps, guide me on this journey of rediscovery. Thank you for your love, grace and mercy. Amen

5
The Common Cure for the Emotionally Malnourished Woman

There is something profound about a simple unintentional gesture that turns into a beautiful moment, changing who you are at your core. Dating and getting to know that special someone should be an exciting time of exploration, along with a chance to turn a moment into a lasting memory. Unfortunately for some men and women, dating and the process of opening themselves up and being vulnerable can cause paralyzing anxiety.

In the beginning of the "getting-to-know-you process," you may feel pressured to say the right thing, make a good impression, wear the right clothing, laugh at jokes that make no sense, and do the best possible job of convincing the other person you're worth date number two. This process can be extremely difficult for someone who is emotionally malnourished and has never experienced unconditional happiness in relationships. Shying away from a gesture as simple as holding hands, declining compliments, or creating conflict where there should be peace are all signs of an emotionally malnourished individual.

When you think of the word "malnourished," you may immediately think of lacking food or nutrients, which equates to starving. Buzzwords like "starving" and "malnourished" send visual images of starving third-world countries scrolling through your mind. On the other hand, being emotionally malnourished involves starvation of the heart and soul. Emotionally malnourished people starve themselves of accepting love because they either feel that they are not worthy or they are unable to trust due to the pain of lingering emotional wounds. If you're unsure about what being emotionally malnourished looks like, let me give you a short preview.

A few years ago, I was dating a gentleman whom I had been involved with for quite some time. To protect the guilty party, I will call him John. Like most of our interactions, the conversations between John and me had become a challenge to continue, and I was no longer interested in what he had to say. During this particular date, I sat on the other side of the room directly across from him, zoning in and out as I watched John's lips move. I would nod every few minutes and say a word or two to acknowledge that I heard what he was saying. Actually, though, I could not have cared less about the vicious nouns, adjectives, and expletives that rolled off John's tongue and escaped his lips because I'd already shut down within the first few moments of his speech.

The point of John's rant was to help me understand how my nonchalant attitude was affecting our relationship. John used words like "mean," "stubborn," and "hard" to describe me. The mirror of revelation John tried to hold in front of my face did not reveal anything new to me. I'd known for a while I could be difficult, unyielding, and damn near impossible to figure out. In high school I learned my inability to make myself emotionally available would ruin future relationships, but somehow I still could not stop myself from swallowing the pill of bitterness.

In my junior year of high school, I developed a crush on the all-American boy next door. Just for the sake of anonymity, we'll call him Tee. At seventeen years old, Tee was damn near perfect in my opinion. He was the captain of the football team, a star basketball player, and a scholar. Tee and I had become great friends after bonding over the absence of our biological fathers. We shared stories of how it felt to be abandoned, as well as the void that was left from not having a relationship with the men who helped to create us. Tee's father had abandoned him and his mother when he was just a baby. Although I knew who my father was, he had never been a part of my life. Unlike Tee, at that point in my life I did not even have a memory of my father and me ever being in the same room together. Being able to honestly share my feelings about my father's absence made me connect with Tee on a level I had not experienced with any of my other friends. I think this connection is what made me feel like Tee was the one.

I made it no secret that I had a crush on Tee, but he rejected me at every turn. Finally, one day I asked him why he didn't like me. Tee told me I was a pretty girl and a great friend, but I was just too mean sometimes. Tee expressed he could not figure out how I could be so nice one minute and then strike like a tiger the next.

While listening to John go on and on about how my attitude was affecting our relationship, I felt like I was experiencing déjà vu. Tee had spoken some of those same words years ago, and nothing had changed. I knew what John was saying to me was true. I did have issues with hypersensitivity, but somehow it seemed I could not change. There seemed to be some invisible force preventing me from accepting love from a man.

The worst feeling in the world is knowing you desperately need to be free, but you have no idea how to unlock the door and escape to freedom. It was like being a dog penned up behind an invisible electric fence. I could walk toward the edge, seeing nothing that would harm me or hinder my progress, but as soon as I took the step to liberation, the invisible fence would shock me back to my reality. Something was blocking me that I could not see with my physical eye, but I could feel it with my emotional heart. The strange thing was the more I liked a guy, the more difficult I became. My behavior baffled me so much that I spent many days and nights trying to figure out what was wrong with me.

While half-listening to John, I tried to convince myself that I would change and improve how I communicated with him. John was a good guy, and he seemed to be honestly attempting to make things work. I tried to talk myself out of responding with a tongue-lashing that would tear John down, but my mouth worked faster than my brain. I looked over at John and simply said, "If you are so unhappy with the way I treat you, then why don't you leave me alone?" As I listened to the words travel through my mouth, I immediately regretted them, but it was too late. The words had escaped my lips and made their way into the atmosphere, so I could not take them back.

I sat in front of John, trying to hold it together. I had just spat verbal acid in his face, and it was too late to back down. In my mind, I could not apologize to him because an apology would just be a sign of weakness. With a furrowed brow and a confused gaze, John tried to figure out what his response would be, but he was speechless. While trying to figure out my next move, I was overwhelmed by feelings of uncertainty and disappointment with my inability to correct myself. I was uncertain about what John's response would be once he got over the initial shock about my boldness. I figured the best thing for me to do was to excuse myself from the room and leave his home.

Even though I was prepared to never hear from him again, he called me a few days later. He shared with me that he thought I was a beautiful woman and a loyal, giving friend, but as a girlfriend I was emotionally unavailable. John explained to me that I reminded him of his mother, who also was emotionally unavailable. For him, something always seemed to be missing from his parents' relationship. Even as a child, he felt his parents were disconnected.

For the first time, I apologized to John and explained to him I had no idea why I could not allow myself to be emotionally available. Then I told him we should stop seeing each other. John told me whenever I did let go of whatever tied me up in knots, I would make someone an excellent wife. The use of the word "wife" made me uncomfortable. Until that moment, I'd never had the desire to be married or have children because I didn't think I was capable of being a good wife or mother.

After John and I broke up, I took a break from dating. I needed to figure out the why, how, when, and what made me so emotionally unavailable. I prayed for God to reveal my weaknesses and insecurities to me. At the recommendation of a friend, I started reading *The Richest Man Who Ever Lived*, by Steven K. Scott. While reading Scott's book, I paid particular attention to the chapter on seeking good counsel.

On the journey to figure out who I was and what made me tick, I encountered a group of exceptional women who would change my life by pouring into me a wealth of wisdom and feeding my malnourished soul. These older women possessed an abundance of professional, relationship, and life experience they freely shared with me. They were honest, raw, nurturing, and encouraging, and I am forever grateful for the blessing of their friendship.

Being in the midst of such good counselors helped me to realize getting involved in a relationship did not have to be that hard. I learned vulnerability, tenderness, and a little ego-stroking does not equate to weakness. On the other hand, being bitter, hard, unyielding, emasculating, and rigid do not equal strength. Instead, emotional strength is being able to say I am hurt, I feel exposed, and I need to be held—if only for a few moments.

Growing up in a single-parent household and having no real model for a healthy relationship forced me to draw my own conclusion of what a relationship should look like. Most of my friends also came from single-parent homes, and most of the married people I knew were going through "married-people drama," which I wanted no part of. The single women I knew were only concerned about material things. They were still into neck rolling and lip poppin', spitting out phrases like "I wish I would . . . ," "All men are dogs," or "I'll never let a man . . ." while always doing the exact opposite. And I grew up around very opinionated women who rarely asked a man for his opinion on anything.

My grandparents were great and I loved them dearly, but I could not glean much from them regarding healthy communication. My grandmother is a very strong woman who has never been afraid to voice her opinion on any subject. However, my grandfather could sit in the same room with you and not open his mouth to utter one word. You can well imagine what their communication as husband and wife was like. I don't regret being exposed to any of these aforementioned situations or personalities, but I wish I had learned sooner rather than later that it's not the way things had to be.

I grew up in the era when parents didn't openly talk to their daughters about boys, sex, and dating. Most of my girlfriends were not allowed to date, so we would all sneak out together on a girls' outing and meet our boyfriends. Everything I learned was from the kids at school and in the streets and Mrs. Mac, my high school health teacher. What I got out of her class was a poorly informed, outdated health film warning me, "Don't let him touch you there." By the time I was a sophomore in high school, several friends I went to elementary school with were having babies of their own. Although this was a normal occurrence in the culture I was exposed to, I knew one thing for sure: I'd better not bring a baby home.

I've always had male friends, and I'm often the only woman sitting at a table full of men. Most of the good, useful information I've learned about relationships has come from watching them make mistakes I don't want to experience myself with a man, as well as letting them give me honest advice that has saved me from a whole lot of drama. In a way, my relationships with my male friends has given me a false sense of who I am as a woman. I had to learn biologically and anatomically I am just that—a woman—and it's okay to act as such. Contrary to popular opinion, women and men are wired differently, so our gender needs are different as well. It's okay to be strong, independent, and tuned in to the games men play, but at the end of the day you have to be sensitive enough to curl up next to that man and be a woman.

There is a difference between independence and stubbornness. For the most part, I grew up watching my mother do everything on her own. She went to work every day to send me to private school. She went to school, paid the bills, shoveled the snow, got the oil changed, and bought cars without consulting a man. In fact, my mother did everything she could without receiving any assistance from a man. Everything seemed to be great in our house, and my mother made sure I wanted for nothing, so what did *I* need a man for? My outside influences taught me men were only good for satisfying a physical need and paying the bills, so I set my mind on being a physically satisfied woman who would always have my lights on.

Now, I'm sure by now some independent woman's head is spinning and pointing her finger yelling, "I make my own money, so I don't need a man." Well, calm down and look around. You're probably sitting in your bed, reading this book alone. Let's be clear about this: there is nothing wrong with being able to earn a living and handle your business as a single woman. The challenge comes when you are so driven you forget that jobs, education, wealth, and red-bottom shoes will not hold your hand when you're old and collecting cats.

When I began my journey to figure out how to feed my emotionally malnourished soul, I discovered the following:

1. My thought process and the way I approached relationships would not allow me to sustain a successful relationship.

2. I could not take past issues into a new relationship.

3. I would have to learn it's okay to be vulnerable.

4. I needed to learn it's okay to trust, but not to be foolish.

5. I needed to hang in there and not run at the first sign of trouble.

6. Don't be so critical; learn to listen before reacting.

7. Stroking a man's ego is not a sign of weakness.

8. I deserve to be happy.

9. I will not lower my standards. It is possible to have what I want without losing myself in the process.

10. I needed to confront and work through whatever had twisted me into emotional knots.

From the day I got my first official boyfriend as a freshman in high school, I have had to teach myself how to successfully function in relationships. Unfortunately on some levels I have failed miserably, but I have learned not to beat myself up over the mistakes I've made. They say we should not live with regrets, but the simple truth is that I regret not confronting the truth about my insecurities sooner. It is insecurity that makes us women put on a full-blown dramatic act and show our behinds when it is so unnecessary. By the time I reached the

5 The Common Cure for the Emotionally Malnourished Woman

point in my life when I was ready to admit to myself that I wanted to be in a real relationship, willing to take the risk and tackle the good, the bad and the ugly, I had no idea what to do. I had been in control for so long I didn't know how to let go—until an awkward moment turned into a beautiful memory.

One day I met a gentleman whom we'll call James to protect the guilty. At the time, I didn't feel confident about taking the chance to get to know someone I knew nothing about. But we were introduced by a mutual friend whom I trusted, so I said, "What the hell." Unfortunately, at the time I met James, I was in the middle of a "leasing" situation, which I'll explain later on. I'd settled into my "only child" syndrome, so I didn't really want to be bothered with anyone. At the same time, I was still open to something new. James lived over fifteen hundred miles away (three hours by plane and twenty-one hours by car), so I wasn't too worried about getting caught up in a serious relationship.

My first encounter with James did not go so well. You guessed it—it was kind of my fault. Needless to say, I had a lot of issues to work out, and it was not the best time for me. James and I communicated sporadically throughout the year, keeping the lines of communication open. As fate would have it, after almost a year of minimal communication, we were scheduled to be in the same city. We spent a few hours hanging out, just talking much about nothing. As a total shock to me, I enjoyed James's company and looked forward to seeing him again.

Before James and I parted for the evening, he reached out to hug me. I'm not sure why his innocent gesture was shocking to me, but it caught me off guard. I had positioned myself to walk behind him, but when he turned to hug me, instead of the side hug that I'm used to giving, I got a little more of James' shoulder and his chest than I had planned. What James meant as a simple departing gesture turned out to be something special.

Hugging James for that brief moment made me feel something I had never felt with any man. For a split second, I felt free—not twisted in knots and anxious. I closed my eyes for a few seconds and allowed myself to let go without reservation. As far back as I could remember, I had never breathed while hugging a man. I was always holding my breath, making sure I was on guard to control the moment.

After James left and the door closed, I stood on the other side with my hand placed over my heart, and exhaled. That was my "aha moment." Walking over to the nearby lounge chair, I realized three things: 1) I was starving for affection, meaning tenderness and a gentle touch . . . not sex; 2) I no longer wanted to be in control; and 3) I was emotionally malnourished. I could finally wrap my arms around that thing that would not allow me to be vulnerable to the *eros* kind of love.

As time passed, I realized that James was not "the one," but he played a significant part in creating a beautiful moment, and I will forever appreciate him for that. From my encounter with James, I learned that it's perfectly fine to be vulnerable. When I open my heart to "the one," I know I will not devour and spit him out like I'd done others. I would not be the overbearing image of stubborn independence and think that a man is just an extra accessory. I would not be selfish and exit stage left at the first sign of boredom. I would give it the best shot I could without compromising my authentic self.

At the end of the day, everyone has a significant amount of baggage they carry. It would be easy to say I was emotionally unavailable because of abandonment issues surrounding my father's absence in my life. I could also blame it on my lack of exposure to healthy relationships growing up or my sexual abuse by Victim. There is a laundry list of factors that played a key role in how I developed emotionally as a child, teenager, and young adult. But as a grown woman, I am responsible for how I live my life, what I accept for myself, and what I give to others. This is my simple advice:

1. **Learn how to be your own woman.** You are not your mother, grandmother, aunt, sister, etc., so let the cycle end with you. Your mother may have been hurt by your father or some other man (men), and now she is bitter and alone because she can't pick up and trust again. You have to learn how to respect where your parents are in their own emotional journey. It's okay to assert your own independence and have a mind of your own while still respecting and honoring your parents' opinions.

2. **Allow bitter women limited access.** Negativity is infectious—it's just that simple. If you spend your Friday nights with your bitter, man-hating single girlfriends or friends who hate their husbands, then I suggest you find a group of positive friends who have a realistic, healthy view of the good, bad, and ugly that comes with relationships.

3. **He is not your daddy.** Most women who grow up without a father in their lives or have strained relationships with their fathers spend too much time and energy trying to make someone else fill the void left by Daddy. The truth is no one can fill that void but your biological father. Unfortunately,

sometimes these rifts in the relationship we desire to have with our fathers will never be repaired. This is a painful and ugly truth, but you have to learn how to push through the pain. It is unfair for you to blame every man who comes into your life for the mistake your father made.

4. **Get yourself a good platonic male friend.** Typically, men are not in competition with other women. There is no need for jealousy, hate, and sabotage between men and women. Men are open and honest with their women friends about the insecurities and unnecessary drama we often display and can't see ourselves. Men see things in us other women either don't see or will never tell us. The flip side is connecting with a platonic male friend can be tricky. If you don't have one already, then chances are they are just hanging out in the friend zone, waiting to be released to midnight-call status.

5. **Seek good counsel.** Never underestimate the power of good girlfriend(s). These are not the women who will tell you what you want to hear, male-bash with you, dislike what you don't like, and agree with everything you say. Instead, they will be honest with you and aren't afraid to call you out when you're wrong. You can have a heated disagreement today but meet for breakfast with them in the morning. Be sure to connect with a diverse group that is composed of women who are professionally and emotionally stable, single, married, engaged, divorced, young, old, and in-between. These are confident women with no other hidden agenda but to help you heal.

6. **Seek professional help.** Some emotional scars are just too deep to handle on your own. If your emotional challenges consume you and render you unable to function in all areas of your life, it is a good idea to consult with a trained professional. A licensed and trained professional can offer you an honest and objective method of working through your issue.

7. **It's okay to be vulnerable.** The key to any healthy relationship is honesty. It's perfectly fine to share your fears with your mate. When you remain distant and rigid with no explanation regarding your behavior, you set your relationship up for failure by leading your partner into the blunder of assumption. Without a clear explanation of why you can't connect, or you fail to acknowledge that there is an issue; people tend to assume that you are just

a bitch. It's a harsh word and an unfair classification, but women who display emotional detachment, sarcasm, the inability to enjoy a simple touch, and other emotional red flags are often viewed that way.

Don't underestimate the power of a man's sensitivity. If he truly and unconditionally loves you, he will support you while you work through your challenges. Being open about what hinders you from connecting emotionally can bridge the gap between your bad attitude and emotional malnourishment.

6
Too Full To Be Blessed

Let me begin this chapter by saying that I am not a relationship expert. I'm not married. I am single, but I am happy. Although it would be great to have someone to share my days and nights with in holy matrimony, my entire existence and happiness does not revolve around finding the perfect man.

As a single woman in ministry, I'm asked at least three times a week, "When are you getting married?" Typically, people think there's something wrong with being single. In fact, many appear to be more concerned about my single status than I am. There is always the ever-popular concerned response from people, "I just want you to be happy." Naturally, I smile and just say thank you, but in my mind I have several questions rattling around in my brain waiting to spill out through my mouth: "What makes you think I'm unhappy? Do I walk around in a black veil, wearing a sign that says 'Somebody, anybody, please marry me?' Does my license plate read 'SPINSTER?' When I walk, do you hear a little clock ticking, counting down how many years I have left before I die of loneliness or my eggs expire?"

There is a misconception that all single women are lonely and desperate to find a mate. Sometimes being single is a choice, not a condition. I am a single woman who's happy. My biological clock is not ticking, and I don't hear wedding bells ringing every second. I'm not religiously reading Scriptures on how to get my Boaz, nor am I writing the name of a man down on a piece of paper and placing it in my Bible next to the verse that refers to marriage. I have not called Miss Cleo and asked her to dip a chicken's foot in a special elixir and pray to the matrimony gods to send me a man.

These are desperate acts to make something happen at your own pace and not in God's time. I am not single because I can't get a man. I am not single because I have incurable halitosis. I am not single because there is something wrong with me the human eye cannot see. I'm not single because I'm a bed-hopper sowing my wild oats . . . I am single simply because . . . I am.

I don't want to confuse you or appear self-righteous; it would be great to experience the joy of being in a healthy, secure relationship with a man who loves me unconditionally. I think every person should want to experience the joy of being in love. However, the important thing to remember is this: you cannot let the status of being single turn into a condition or a brand.

After my experience with James, the gentleman you met in a previous chapter, I made the decision to take a break from dating. At the time, I needed to be single. I took a long, hard look at myself—my thought process, my choices in men, and the way I was operating in my professional, personal, and spiritual life—and I knew the way I felt about myself and saw myself would not support a healthy relationship. Of course, when I expressed this to people who inquired about the reasons why I was single, their response was, "That's B.S." Most people feel the explanations, "I'm working on myself," or "I'm focusing on my career" are just excuses for feeling good about being single. For some, those statements might very well be a haphazard attempt to explain why they are single when they have a strong desire to be a plus-one. For me, though, this was simply the truth.

When I mentioned reading Scriptures and writing your desired mate's name down and placing it in the Bible, of course I was being a bit facetious. Philippians 4:6-8 says, "Be anxious for nothing, but in everything by prayer and supplication, with thanksgiving, let your requests be made known to God; and the peace of God, which surpasses all understanding, will guard your hearts and minds through Christ Jesus."

If you're reading this chapter and finding yourself unable to connect because you cannot find happiness as a single woman, you're probably saying, "I've prayed for a man, so why am I still single?" Being a Christian and dating can often be frustrating and confusing. We believe if we just keep praying, God will send us a mate. We pray for God to send us a mate, and 24 hours after our prayer has left our lips, we meet a man on aisle 6 of the grocery store. Desperation leads us to believe that God has blessed us with *the one*—our Boaz.

If you are unhappily single and feel a man will help fill that void, actually you could already be too full for God to bless you. You are too full with the regret of past relationships, unforgiveness, and bitterness. You can't let go of a man who hurt you ten years ago. You are unable to give or receive true love because you don't completely understand what love looks like or feels like. You are afraid to trust because you don't want to risk getting hurt, cast aside, or abandoned. You are too full with trash from your past, so God needs to empty you to bless you.

Right now you might be in a familiar place; unfortunately, holding on to trash has become so familiar to you it's comfortable. No matter how toxic it is, you have settled into a place that has you convinced a relationship will complete you and solve all your problems. Yet, you keep entering into relationships, picking up more trash.

Step back and take a moment to thoroughly examine every area of your life. Look at your dating patterns and think about the men whom you've allowed to make deposits into your emotional trashcan just to remove the brand of being single. Proverbs 18:22 (KJV) says, "Whosoever findeth a wife findeth a good thing, and obtaineth favour of the Lord." God wants to prepare you for *His* best—not what you perceive to be the perfect man. So, seek Him as your guide to navigate through this season of singleness.

The story of Ruth and Boaz, which takes place in the Book of Ruth, is one of the most familiar love connections in the Bible, and has become such a hot topic today that it's the subject of books, poems, social media postings, and sermons. In fact, Ruth and Boaz's love story has sent many women in search of that *perfect* love.

The Book of Ruth is tucked between Judges and 1 Samuel. Since Ruth has only four chapters, if you're thumbing through the Bible too fast, you just might miss it. Most people miss the intricately woven tale of restoration, faith, obedience, trust, and hope and dive right into the romance. There's not enough space on these pages for me to dig into this book and explore it in its entirety. For now, I will merely scratch the surface of the story of Ruth and Boaz. (If you would like to study this Bible book further, read *Finding Fullness Again*, by Dr. Ralph Douglas West. In this insightful book, he walks you through the story of Ruth, allowing you to appreciate this story about how God blesses faithfulness.)

The Book of Ruth begins with background on Naomi, Ruth's mother-in-law, and how she and Ruth are connected. Ruth was married to one of Naomi's sons. After losing her husband and both sons, Naomi was left with no immediate family, so she decided to move back to her home of Bethlehem. Upon making this decision, Naomi encouraged a young and vibrant Ruth to move on with her life, assuring her she would find another husband. But Ruth refused to leave Naomi, expressing it this way: "Where you go I will go, and where you stay I will stay. Your people will be my people and your God my God" (1:16).

After returning to Bethlehem with her daughter-in-law by her side, Naomi knew it was time for them to move forward with their lives. Being widowed, the two women had no means of support and no husbands to care for them, so they would now have to find the means to support themselves.

Ruth suggested to Naomi that she go out into a field to gather leftover grain from anyone who showed her favor. It was the custom in those times for widows to be permitted to gather grain in the fields to prepare bread for their table. This would allow the widows who had no means of support to have food to eat. While Ruth was gathering grain, a man named Boaz, who was also a relative of Naomi's, noticed her and inquired about her. After learning that Ruth was Naomi's daughter-in-law, Boaz told Ruth that she could glean in his field, and he ordered no one to bother her. Ruth wondered why Boaz would show such kindness to her. What Ruth didn't know was that the news of her reputation for faithfulness to God and loyalty to Naomi had spread around town.

Born a Moabite, Ruth did not worship God; instead, she worshiped a god called Chemosh. But through her connection to Naomi, she had come to know and love God the Father. Boaz told Ruth that he admired her loyalty to Naomi and wanted to repay her kindness by putting bread on her table. Boaz instructed the overseers to not only allow Ruth to gather grain in his field, but to also leave a little grain behind just for Ruth. In these first few passages, I learned **Lesson #1:**

Loyalty. Ruth displayed a key character quality for any relationship—loyalty. By refusing to leave Naomi and return to her ways and beliefs as a Moabite, Ruth not only showed loyalty to Naomi, but to God as well. Loyalty is important in any relationship. Your mate wants the reassurance that you will have his back and not run at the first sign of trouble. Loyalty says "even though I might not know our destination, I trust you enough to follow."

As we continue reading this book, we learn Ruth gleaned in the field all day and gathered more than enough to feed her and Naomi. The Scripture passage says Ruth's harvest was equal to an ephah, or thirty pounds. While gleaning in the field, Boaz made sure Ruth was taken care of, providing her with water when she was thirsty and food when she was hungry. When Ruth returned home, Naomi was overwhelmed by the amount of harvest Ruth had gathered. Ruth recounted the acts of kindness shown to her by Boaz. Naomi praised God for the blessing of Boaz and then informed her daughter-in-law that Boaz was a close relative. The King James Version refers to Boaz as a kinsman, a relative who could come to the rescue of another relative on the brink of financial ruin.

The kindness and interest Boaz had shown to Ruth lent hope to Naomi. She knew Boaz was smitten with Ruth. In a classic move that most successful matchmakers have mastered, Naomi encouraged Ruth to continue to gather in Boaz's field. Naomi knew Ruth would be safe and no harm would come to her. Naomi also recognized that Boaz was good husband material. Naomi knew as a man of God, Boaz would provide and care for Ruth. Boaz was financially stable and a man of good character. Here we find our **second lesson...**

Position yourself. Most women get caught up in celebrating that Ruth got her man, but they miss one key move by Ruth. Ruth positioned herself to be noticed by Boaz. One thing you must realize is when praying for God to send you a mate, you can't just sit around and wait for a man to fall out of the sky and land on the couch next to you. God is not a magician who will wave a magic wand that will make John Doe appear. Ruth was hungry, so she didn't sit in the house waiting on someone to knock on the door and hand her a basket full of grain. Instead, she went out and worked for it. In the middle of her hard work, she was rewarded. Ruth positioned herself to reveal yet another one of her great attributes, her willingness to work hard when times got tough.

As time passed and Ruth continued to glean in Boaz's field, Naomi finally knew the time was right. One day Naomi instructed Ruth to go to the threshing floor where Boaz would be working to ensure the grain gathered was sifted and unwanted seeds and waste were eliminated. This was a place where women typically did not go, especially at night alone. Pay close attention to the instructions given by Naomi and Ruth's response to the instruction.

> "My daughter, I must find a home for you, where you will be well provided for. Now Boaz, with whose women you have worked, is a relative of ours. Tonight he will be winnowing barley on the threshing floor. Wash, put on perfume, and get dressed in your best clothes. Then go down to the threshing floor, but don't let him know you are there until he has finished eating and drinking. When he lies down, note the place where he is lying. Then go and uncover his feet and lie down. He will tell you what to do." "I will do whatever you say," Ruth

answered. So she went down to the threshing floor and did everything her mother-in-law told her to do.

(Ruth 3:1-6 NIV)

There are two lessons to be learned . . .

1) Seek good counsel. Most single women make the mistake of relying on misguided information from other single women who are bitter because they are single. Whether you are married or single, you should always surround yourself with positive people. If you are single and miserable, talking to other women who are unlucky in love may cause you to continue to snuggle up to a bottle of wine, drowning your loneliness in Moscato more nights than you wish to count. As a single woman seeking a healthy relationship, I sought the advice and guidance of mature women who had healthy long-lasting marriages and relationships. After years of having an unhealthy view of relationships and being emotionally unavailable, I wanted a raw and uncut version of the good, bad, and the ugly from women who still maintained a sense of personal independence, but respected their husband's position as the priest of the household.

2) Prepare yourself. Naomi instructed Ruth to prepare herself to go and meet Boaz. In those ancient times, it was customary to prepare for special events and ceremonies by cleansing your body and clothing yourself in clean garments and scented oils. This was a purifying ritual that cleansed you spiritually to prepare for a deeper relationship with God. Ruth prepared herself before she visited Boaz. She treated her body and spirit as a bride would for her groom. Ruth was not just going to see Boaz to engage in idle chitchat. She wasn't going to the threshing floor to drop off a batch of corn bread and butter beans for a midnight snack. She wasn't going so Boaz could see how good she looked in her new outfit. Ruth was about serious business when she went to the threshing floor; in fact, she had prepared herself to receive the blessing of marriage.

Before Ruth offered herself as a bride, though, she prepared herself by cleansing away the trash she had been carrying around with her. She cleansed herself of life as a mourning widow, the uncertainty of moving to a foreign land, and her status of a Moabite non-believer. In other words, Ruth removed the emotional trash that would hinder her from being a good helpmate.

Today sometimes we get so caught up in the ceremony we miss the service. Being a wife is more than having a platinum wedding, wearing a ring, and having someone whom you can refer to as husband. Being a wife involves a God-ordained relationship covenant between you and the man God has created for you. Take this time as a single woman to prepare yourself by cleansing your mind and emotions of the clutter keeping you from seeing that you are worthy of being truly loved—not as a side piece, a temporary fix, or a lease without an option to buy, but as a wife or committed partner.

As single women, we spend quite a bit of time trying to figure out if a man is worthy of being with us. We always ask the question, "What does he bring to the table?" It is time, however, to start asking ourselves, "What am I bringing to the table?" We should always ask ourselves, "Am I bringing all my trash, and expecting him to clean it up? Am I bringing my ex-husband's abuse? Am I bringing my ex-boyfriend's cheating? Am I bringing my father's abandonment? Am I bringing the insecurity of not being worthy of being loved? Instead, am I allowing God to clean me up to prepare me for His blessing?"

> "This kindness is greater than that which you showed earlier: You have not run after the younger men, whether rich or poor. And now, my daughter, don't be afraid. I will do for you all you ask. All the people of my town know that you are a woman of noble character."
>
> (Ruth 3: 9-11)

In this passage **lesson five** is revealed; **Try something different**. Although Boaz was able to care for Ruth, he was not the only kinsman in town who could marry her. A good physical description of Boaz is not provided, so there is no indication he was as handsome as King David. Ruth 3:10 reveals that Boaz was significantly older than Ruth. In my mind I see Boaz as one of those old-school smooth men with an irresistible swagger and kindness that cancels out any imperfections. Ruth was a young and vibrant woman who was capable of catching the eye of any eligible bachelor of her choice. There were other men in Bethlehem who met the same criteria as Boaz, but Ruth wanted him. Today we often get so caught up in what we think our type is that we overlook a "diamond in the rough." I'd like to think Boaz had the swagger factor.

When I was a teenager, I was attracted to anyone my mother did not approve of. When I was in my twenties, physical attraction ruled my dating world. If he was fine with a gorgeous face, he was my type. But in my thirties, I became smitten with swagger. "Swagger" means different things to different people. Typically for me, swagger is not necessarily how a man looks physically, but instead he has that something that makes him stand out from the rest. Unlike in my twenties, I am now attracted to a man who loves and serves God faithfully, and strong but sensitive enough to listen and comfort me in my moments of vulnerability. I am stimulated by intellect, so I like a man who starts a conversation with, "I was reading this book and . . ." I also like a man who enjoys the sounds of Miles Davis, but can also rock with me at an old-school 8 Ball and MJG concert. I like a man who understands my independence does not threaten his manhood. I like a man who is secure and understands that just because I speak to another man in the grocery store, I only have eyes for him.

If you are focused on a particular type, there is a possibility you could be missing out on something special. By no means am I telling you to lower your standards or settle for someone you know in your heart you will not be happy with just for the sake of being in a relationship. I am encouraging you to look beneath the surface and open your eyes to what is in his heart. Sometimes God's blessings don't come in the form you've requested, but He always knows what's best.

> So she lay at his feet until morning, but got up before anyone could be recognized; and he said, "No one must know that a woman came to the threshing floor." He also said, "Bring me the shawl you are wearing and hold it out." When she did so, he poured into it six measures of barley and placed the bundle on her. Then he went back to town.
>
> (Ruth 3:14-15 NIV)

Lesson six; Respect and Protection. Most women are attracted to a man with a little edge—someone who can offer them excitement and adventure. Along with excitement, adventure, and swagger, good character is a must. In Ruth 3:14-15, Boaz protects Ruth's reputation. Every move Boaz has made proves he is a man of noble character. When Boaz saw Ruth gleaning in the fields, he immediately knew he wanted to care for her the best way he could at that moment. His instinct as a protector kicked in, so he wanted to make sure she was in a safe area.

When she traveled to the threshing floor, Ruth had no business there at night surrounded by predators. The threshing floor was dirty and staffed with men who might not have been as respectful as Boaz. If caught on the threshing floor, Ruth could be perceived as a groupie, an opportunist waiting to catch the eye of an available man. Being at the threshing floor was not a good place for Ruth to be seen. Before traveling to the threshing floor, Ruth and Naomi knew she was taking a risk and Ruth should not be seen by anyone other than Boaz. Ruth and Naomi knew they could trust Boaz and he would treat Ruth with respect. In verse 14, Boaz tells Ruth no one should know she has been at the threshing floor. In other words, he didn't want to put her business in the street and ruin her reputation of being a woman of noble character.

Just as Boaz had provided for Ruth while gleaning in the field, he also made sure she did not leave the threshing floor empty handed. He gave her enough barley for both her and her mother-in-law to eat. In today's social climate of groupies, gold-diggers, and opportunists, dating has been reduced to a layaway plan. Men make payments on women while deciding if they want to keep them or not. A number of women are centering their worth on the price a man pays for them. But Boaz didn't just throw cheap trinkets at Ruth to satisfy her. Instead, Boaz had a plan for Ruth.

When you are trying to catch the eye of a man with deep pockets, there is one important thing you should know about him: just because he has money does not mean he will freely give it to you. For most men who are considered *rich*, a few car note payments, a couple of handbags and few boxes of shoes, and a light bill here and there is just a maintenance fee paid for services rendered. There is no real investment or plan of commitment.

With our increased dependence on social media, we broadcast our business for everyone to see. People post about break-ups, infidelity, and other information that should be kept between couples and not for the world to weigh in on. Boaz was not concerned with his buddies knowing that Ruth had sneaked down to the threshing floor to see him. He didn't run off and say, "Yeah man, last night I had her lying at my feet." Boaz kept his mouth shut and kept their business between them. Boaz wanted to make sure that Ruth's reputation stayed intact and she was taken care of. He made sure that she had food on her table that fed her entire household. Ruth was more than just beautiful arm candy for him; instead, she was a virtuous woman who was worthy of being courted and respected.

In Ruth 4, Boaz keeps his promise to Ruth. He meets with the eligible elders in the community who can also serve as her guardian-redeemer. Honoring the law of the land, Boaz puts his cards on the table and basically says to them, "Hey, I'm interested in Ruth and I'm ready to make an honest woman of her, but because I don't want any drama and it's the right thing to do, I'm checking with you guys to see what's up." Fortunately for Boaz, the other guardian-redeemers had no interest in marrying Ruth and acquiring the property that would accompany her upon marriage.

After getting the green light, Boaz announced to the whole town that Ruth was his girl and he wanted to marry her. There was no ambiguity, no room for Ruth to try and figure out where she stood with Boaz. If a man has long-term plans for you to be in his life, he will make his intentions clear and leave no room for you to wonder where you stand. If you find yourself asking, "What are we doing?" or "Where are we going?" it's possible that you're just being leased.

The Book of Ruth is an intricately woven tale about more than just a relationship between a man and a woman. Ruth is a story of God's reward for obedience. Ruth stepped out on faith to trust God—not a god, but the *living* God. Ruth's quest to be redeemed by someone other than a man led her down the path to receive the ultimate blessing: Her lineage is linked to royalty. Ruth is the great-grandmother of King David. If you crawl further down the family tree, you will see that Ruth is linked to the King of Kings, Jesus Christ. Ruth's obedience put her in direct relationship to Jesus Christ.

Like you, Ruth had to be emptied. She had to lose a husband and leave her family and homeland. She had to stop worshiping *a god* and believe in *the God*. She had to be stripped of everything that seemed familiar and move to a place where she could heal and be blessed with what God wanted her to have.

Ruth's story of faith in the face of the uncertain or unknown is no different from the story of millions of women who share a similar story. At some point in the middle of your own story, you have to make a choice: you can either choose to hoard trash from a painful past and continue engaging in unhealthy relationships, or you can trust God and know that no matter how difficult, your faithfulness to Him and the plan He has for you and your future mate will prevail. Even those of us who believe in Jesus often don't believe Him enough to trust Him. A good friend of mine once said, "It's not enough to believe in God; you have to believe Him." In the same ways, believe He will bless you with a mate whom He has designed for you.

7
Leased Without an Option To Buy

Relationships of any kind are often like entering into a rental or leasing agreement. Sometimes, we allow people to treat us like rental and leasing services. The most common reason people rent cars is to prevent their own vehicles from incurring any unnecessary mileage or wear and tear. Some of us rent cars because we are unsure if the car we own is reliable enough to handle a long trip. Most rental car companies allow unlimited mileage, which means we can take long trips without worrying about accumulating excessive mileage on what we own. Basically, the car is not ours, so we have no real interest in making an investment toward ownership. If we're tired of driving what we own and want to try something new, we just rent a temporary fix. When we are done with a rental, we can return it dirty, worn, and empty and only have to pay a small service fee. Unfortunately, we allow people to treat us, as a lease without an option to buy.

A few years ago when I moved back to Houston from Detroit, I rented a car for a while until my car could be shipped. I drove the leased car around town, incurring mileage and driving carelessly through dirt and over potholes because it was a rental. I could return it without worrying about the consequences of my haphazard use of something I had no vested interest in. Unfortunately, someone hit the side of the rental car and took off without taking responsibility for their actions. I called the rental company, and they instructed me to return the car. I filled out an incident report, gave them the keys, and signed for a replacement—as easy as one-two-three. I left the car used and abused so that someone else would have to deal with my mess.

Just as I irresponsibly handled something I understood to be temporary from the start, we also allow people to ride us until we are broken and have nothing left to give. When we are exhausted and can't go another mile, we are traded in for a newer, more reliable model without a second thought. Sometimes we give of ourselves for selfish reasons. We hope the more we give to someone, the more he or she will realize how much we are truly worth. When dealing with relationships and matters of the heart, we continue to give of ourselves, hoping we will be his or her one and only, but all the while we are only being leased with no option to buy.

We often watch our loved ones love someone or something more than us, but we make excuses for them: they are just working too hard, they are just too busy right now, or they're texting me because they're just too busy with work to talk. There is a number-one rule you should always remember, however: people make time for things and individuals that are important to them—bottom line.

Leasing sounds like a great opportunity with no real commitment, but there is always fine print or a clause that holds you responsible in some way. In the case of the car I rented, at some point I was held responsible for the damage caused to the rental. Of course, I was given another car to drive, yet there were consequences for my abuse, even though I had no vested interest in the car or not considered it an option to purchase.

Likewise, in relationships, the consequence of allowing ourselves to be leased is that during this period, our value is depreciating at the hands of someone else who has no interest in making a long-term investment. When someone else comes along, ready to make a committed investment, we give him or her something used, depreciated, and in dire need of repair. After all the wear and tear, there is nothing left, so we are forced to wear an invisible sign (e.g. "Jane's Lease and Salvage") that only relationship scavengers can read, causing us to be leased over and over again.

Just in case you are getting lost in my metaphors about leasing agreements and car rentals, let me give you a few things to ponder.

Proposed Leasing Options

Texting. Someone reading this book is involved in a relationship that is solely based on texting. There is no real communication between the two of you. Plans to spend quality time together hardly ever become a reality. When you do hear from them, it is always to fulfill a need they have, while you convince yourself your needs are being met as well. If you are reading this book, then most likely you are a grown woman because texting is what children and adolescents do.

Relationships are built upon verbal and visual communication. You need to hear the sound of the other person's voice and see his or face to truly connect because the personal touch cannot be replaced by technology. Although texting is convenient and can quickly answer a question or solve a problem you cannot verbally address right away, it is an impersonal form of communication that cannot produce any real fruit. If you are involved in a relationship in which your communication is solely built on texting, there are a few things to consider. 1) He is just not that into you; 2) He has a girlfriend or significant other, and he's texting you because he's *talking* to her; 3) He has serious communication issues, so he might think texting is okay, which needs to be addressed quickly because communication can make or break a relationship; or 4) As a secret agent, he's being protected by Olivia Pope, so any communication outside of texting could put you in danger. Okay, that last one was a stretch, but if you believe that other hogwash he's selling you, why not believe this? Whether he's too busy with work or allegedly being guarded by witness protection, you are being leased.

The Single Married Man. A single married man is a married man with single-man habits. Ladies, this is really a no-brainer. In fact, there is no need to spend too much time on this one. Some of you are being leased to pay a light bill, and some of you are being leased to support a lifestyle. Nonetheless, you are being leased.

The Sex Prep. This late-night creep has been around even before the Commodores broke up. It comes in different forms. The most common is that phone call you only get when he needs to have sex. That's simple . . . . no explanation is needed. The next one is a little tricky. This call might come the day before he wants to see you, or if he is a long distance away, a week before he arrives in town. This call usually starts with light conversation and chatter that will make you think he just wants to catch up or see how you're doing. Somewhere along the way, the words "I miss you," or "Let's hang out" are thrown in. "Hang Out" is a buzzword phrase for having a few drinks, engaging in more light conversation, and then moving to the bedroom. You should also be aware that the word "friend" is a safe word that cannot be associated with the title "girlfriend." "Friend" simply means you understand that friends "hang out"—and nothing more. At any rate, hanging out usually means you are being leased.

The Friend Zone. The friend zone is often a lonely, confusing, and frustrating place to be. You want more, but he only wants to be your (here's that word again) "friend." The friend zone keeps his needs met. He can "hang out" with you, get advice about his real girlfriend, have a few laughs, and tell you all about his problems while maintaining a friendship because he does not want to ruin the relationship with you. Keep in mind, the friend zone does not exclude sex, and it can often be passed off as a benefit—hence, "friend with benefits." Now, I just gave you a two-for-one. Whether you have fallen into the friend zone or you're a friend with benefits, you are being leased.

The Wishing Well. Leasing doesn't just happen in male/female relationships, but also occurs in friendships and family relationships. You might be that uncle, aunt, or cousin who always comes to the rescue, but when you're dangling on a tight rope, there is no one to catch you. Your friends and family treat you like a wishing well in which they deposit all their penny hopes and nickel dreams, hoping you can make something out of nothing.

On some levels, leasing benefits both parties. When I was in college, I was enamored with a guy we'll call Joe. The first time I saw Joe, I just had to know his name. I met Joe at a step show, where we were formally introduced by one of his fraternity brothers. When he came out on stage and removed his shirt, I almost passed out. (Joe was and still is fine as cat hair. I've always been a sucker for a fine man, but I digress.) My friend—whom we'll call Sharon—and I were sitting next to each other, and all the girls around us were going crazy over Joe. Sharon leaned over and said that she was going to find Joe and talk to him. I told her I would get him first. Sharon and I bet each other twenty dollars that the other would get to Joe first. But I wasn't worried about meeting Joe because I had an inside connection. After the show, I found Joe's line brother Jim and told him I wanted to meet Joe. Jim liked my best friend, so of course I had a bargaining chip. Jim introduced me to Joe, and I left the show with Joe's phone number and twenty bucks. For most of my college life and beyond, Joe and I "hung out." Years later that is what our relationship was classified as—"hanging out."

Before I move forward, I must say Joe is a good guy. He's a great friend to his friends, a good son, and an excellent father. Joe is a hard worker, and he is also very intelligent. During the course of our entire relationship, however, I personally don't feel Joe was the friend to me that I was to him. When I use the word "friend," I mean a genuine "ride-or-die" friend. If there is one thing about me, I can always separate the roles of friend and love interest. If you need me to ride out, I'm there—no matter what—and we can sort out the details of our love life later. In Joe's case, I was the one to whom he would call and tell all his problems. I was always willing to lend him an ear or shoulder to cry on. Joe, on the other hand, was consistently inconsistent.

One of my most memorable moments with Joe was being informed that he had been seeing another girl. When confronted, Joe admitted he was seeing someone else and gave an explanation of his behavior, which was classic Joe. Joe and I broke up, and he left my apartment and went on his way. After leaving my house and arriving at his home, Joe called and asked me if I could drive him to his dentist appointment. At the time, I was livid that he would have the nerve to ask me for a favor after he showed his behind a half-hour earlier. No, I didn't take Joe to the dentist, and we broke up (for a brief minute). Sometimes, when I think of that incident with Joe, I can't help but laugh at the foolishness of it all.

I have countless Joe stories, but I'll keep them to myself. Joe and I lived in this vicious cycle that could not be broken. We would be thick as thieves for a period of time, then we would break up and disconnect for long periods of time without communication. With the evolution of new technology, there was always a line of communication that Joe would cross. After Joe and I had one of our spats, I would always end the conversation with, "Don't call me, don't e-mail me, don't text me, and don't contact me ever again." Yet, despite my ultimatums, Joe would always come back into my life.

My relationship with Joe was wearing thin and had become a huge burden. I was disappointed in myself because I kept leaving the door open for him to walk back through. I told myself that I was just doing it to be a true friend, but the truth was that just as Joe was leasing me, I was leasing him. In my own dysfunctional way, I enjoyed the attention Joe was giving me.

One year Joe and I had planned to see each other while I was in town for a football game. Prior to the game, Joe and I had been communicating again, and I was once again drawn back into the Kiffany and Joe show. As usual, our time together began with our usual drama. It was difficult to enjoy being with old friends and have a great time while dealing with my Joe issues. At the end of the weekend, my friends and I were preparing to leave, and Joe and I were yet again locked in a dramatic tug-of-war. When Joe got in his car to leave, my good friend, who is always brutally honest with me, asked me why I was still wasting my time with Joe. Up until that point, she had never met Joe, even though she had heard numerous accounts of our dysfunctional relationship. This time, she was able to see us in action first hand. She told me that no matter how much he frustrated me, I still liked the attention, but I needed to release both Joe and myself from the unhealthy relationship.

I stood in the middle of the parking lot listening to her talk and watching as Joe drove away. After seeing his car disappear around the corner, I looked at her and told her she was right. At that moment, I realized I was as much to blame for our dysfunctional behavior as Joe was. I allowed Joe to continuously take and give nothing because the more I gave, the more he would stick around and provide me with all the attention I needed. (Sometimes we feel negative attention is better than nothing.)

I have not spoken to Joe in a few years. I wish Joe well and success in every area of his life; but my lease with Joe has expired, and there is no option for renewal.

It is my firm belief that we were made to progress and not remain stagnant or continuously regress. People and things, whatever they may be, serve various purposes in our lives and sometimes they are only meant to be with us for a season—however long that season may last. It's okay to break free from whatever binds you to another person who has no vested interest in you, instead leasing you without an option to buy.

You might be in a situation where you feel used and abused and have no real sense of what you are truly worth. The good news is there is someone who has no interest in leasing you because He has already paid the price—just for you. God created you to be more than just a convenient option. God, in His infinite wisdom, can see things that we cannot and may never see. We see ourselves as unworthy of a real investment, yet He sees us as worthy enough to make us in His own image, worthy of the ultimate investment—His love!

8
What Will You Do with One String?

Depression, even in the pronunciation of the word, feels like you're slowly letting the air out of a tire. A slow and unsettling deflation manifests in the spirit of someone battling depression. Depression carries a stigma related to emotional instability and brokenness. For some of us, bouts of depression are related to situations that greatly affect our ability to experience joy in any area of our lives. Clinical depression is the most common case among people.

Situational depression can be caused by financial strain, failed relationships, death of a loved one, an illness, job-related stress, and countless other challenges that negatively shape our lives. Whatever the cause of depression, it can be both paralyzing and embarrassing. It is difficult for most people to admit to their friends and family they are experiencing bouts of depression.

For Christians, dealing with depression can be especially difficult to cope with. We live in a society that sensationalizes "feel-good religion." In a culture where morals and values have taken a back seat to materialism, popularity, and success at any cost, we feel an overwhelming urge to stay on top. Instead of turning to sound biblical teaching, we tune in to cookie-cutter motivational messages that tell us to "think ourselves happy" and speak positive affirmations that will miraculously fix our brokenness. The truth is, being a Christian does not exempt you from depression. When you study your Bible, you don't have to search hard to find someone who did not experience what has now been diagnosed as depression. In Psalm 42:6 (KJV), David wrote, "O my God, my soul is cast down within me." King David, who was a man after God's own heart, wrote entire psalms while in the throes of depression.

According to www.webmd.com, major depression (clinical depression) is described as a constant state of hopelessness and despair. Yet while David is living in what appears to be a desolate place and his soul is cast down, he still places his hope in God. In verse 11, he declares, "Hope thou in God: for I shall yet praise him, who is the health of my countenance, and my God." Even in David's time of hopelessness, he continues to put his faith in God.

David knew what all Christians should know: Hope is a simple four-letter word that holds miraculous power. Hope can make the difference between success and failure, fruitfulness and barrenness, and hope and hopelessness.

One of the most powerful allegorical adaptations of hope is George Frederic Watts' oil painting that is simply titled "Hope." This nineteenth-century painting depicts a young woman sitting on top of what appears to be the world, wearing a tattered, weather-beaten garment. Her hem is frayed, and her dress has begun to unravel. Hope's clothes carry the remnants of the situation or circumstance that has placed her there alone. She sits with matted hair and her eyes covered by a blood-stained blindfold, holding tightly to a harp that has only one string left. With one hand, she grips the harp and plays that lone string with the other hand as if it were the sweetest sound ever heard. With contorted limbs hunched over the harp holding on to that one string, Hope sits on top of the world alone with no friends, no family, no husband, and no children. In a world filled with silence and despair, the sound of that one string drowns out the sounds of her hopes and dreams crashing around her. Even though Hope only has one string left, she plays that string until she can play no more.

The irony of this painting is that Hope's position suggests she should have everything she needs to be happy. What better place to be than sitting on top of the world? Most of us are in Hope's position, appearing to be in control because our outward appearance and professional and/or financial status all point to happiness—not hopelessness. Like Hope, many of us sit on top of the world holding our position while trying to maintain our footing, while just holding on to that one string.

This painting has inspired sermons on hope and encouragement, including the famous sermon preached by Reverend Jeremiah Wright that inspired President Barack Obama to pen his memoir, *The Audacity of Hope*. Some critics who have dissected Watts' allegorical symbol of hope have concluded that a more appropriate title for the painting would be "Despair." But what is hope without despair? Despair does not mean depletion. Instead, this seemingly negative emotional state challenges us to look beyond the blindfolded darkness and confusion and fix our sights on that symbol of hope in the painting. Indeed, although we are often playing life's dreary tune with one note from one string, there is still hope. Hope's symbol is that one string, which serves as a source of comfort while she sits on top of a world that has abandoned her and dealt her a bad hand—waiting on the day when a change would come.

This painting is especially poignant to me because I can remember several moments in my life when I was sitting on top of the world—alone, scared, and depressed. Meanwhile, I was playing that one string, holding on to nothing but the hope that God would intervene and deliver me from my hopelessness.

In my sophomore year of college, I was diagnosed with Graves' Disease, an autoimmune disorder that causes hyperactivity of the thyroid gland. I had developed a growth on my thyroid gland called a goiter. This was the beginning of a roller coaster ride that would affect me physically and stretch me emotionally farther than I cared to go. There I was, on the verge of a budding career in radio and enjoying college life to the fullest, when the disease struck.

Before I was diagnosed with Graves' Disease, I'd been experiencing bouts with depression and anxiety. My hair was falling out, and my skin was dry and scaly. I was always hoarse, and walking across the room left me panting and out of breath. Due to chronic heart palpitations, I was placed on heart medication until my condition could be regulated. Something was seriously wrong with me, but I had no idea what was happening to my mind and body.

My endocrinologist advised me that I would need radiation treatments to shrink the goiter. After the radiation treatment, however, I developed hypothyroidism, which meant my thyroid was now underactive and I would have to take medication for the rest of my life. The short and sweet of it is, I no longer have a thyroid gland. To function normally every day, I rely on a tiny pill in a bottle that sits on my bathroom counter to make my body work properly.

Unfortunately, since my diagnosis, my life has changed. Just in case you don't know what a thyroid does, let me enlighten you. Your thyroid gland affects all the organs in your body by regulating at what rate they should be working. In the summer of 2004, my thyroid (or lack thereof) told my body to shut down. Working ridiculous hours under extreme stress, I wasn't sleeping at night or eating right, and I wasn't taking my medication daily as prescribed. I had stretched my body to the point of no return, and my organs were working overtime trying to function properly. A visit to my doctor revealed that my TSH and T4 levels were six times higher than normal. At the end of my doctor's appointment, I went home with a month off work, a prescription for heart medication, and blood pressure meds. I spent my time off work trying to recuperate, but unfortunately my body had been pushed to the limit, and I would have to fight harder to recover. My month off work turned into two years of battling one symptom after another.

Ironically, the physical toll of weakened heart muscles, high blood pressure, hand tremors, and extreme fatigue was minimal compared to the emotional and psychological warfare that I would experience over a period of two years. Because I was sick and could not properly take care of myself, I moved back to Detroit with my mother. I did not work and had no insurance to help cover my medical expenses. I was sick, broke, and depressed.

I spent most of my days closed up in the house, wishing I was somewhere else. I felt like my life was interrupted and my independence stripped. I was Hope, sitting on top of the world surrounded by hopelessness and despair, desperately holding on to one string.

While still living in Houston, there was a moment in time when I thought my illness had developed into some type of psychosis I could not avoid or understand. Before I packed up and left for Detroit, I started thinking about people I'd never met and had no idea how I knew them. I started seeing images of people without faces. These people's lives played out in my head like vivid images from a movie scene.

A few weeks after I'd settled in Detroit, I woke up one morning drenched in sweat. My heart was beating fast, and I felt like I was suffocating. My stomach started to hurt, and the room began to spin. I was scared because I thought I was having a heart attack. I called for my mother, but she had already left for work. I got out of bed and fell to my knees. I crawled from my bedroom to the bathroom. While on my knees, I started taking off my sweat-soaked clothes. Lying on the cold bathroom floor naked, I tried to figure out what was going on for over an hour. After I figured out I wasn't going to die, I got up from the floor and took a shower. While I was in the shower, I prayed and cried. Even after my shower, I prayed and cried all day, begging the Lord to deliver me from whatever hell I was going through. I prayed so hard I felt like my lips were vibrating.

After praying, the name of Paul kept flashing through my mind. Thinking of Paul from the Bible, I started reading 2 Corinthians. In 2 Corinthians 12:1-9, Paul begged for God to remove his thorn, but the

Lord said no. Paul became a great source of comfort to me, and he helped me understand what I was going through.

After entering a season of constant prayer, the thought entered my head that I should start writing a book. I had attempted several times to do this, but I was too busy living life to give it too much attention. At that point in my life, however, I had all the time in the world, so it was the perfect time to start writing. As it turned out, those people I saw and heard in the early stages of my illness were characters in my first book, *The Green-Eyed Butterfly*.

Over the next few months, the characters and I would become bonded forever. The main character, Seth St. James and I were so closely knit together that sometimes it was difficult to determine where I began and she ended. For two years, that terrible period I lived in despair and sickness would be spent writing the first two installments of the Seth St. James series, along with a third book entitled *Bitter Honey* and the first draft of *Beautiful Lies*.

While I was sitting on top of the world in the midst of hopelessness, begging for God to remove the thorn of physical sickness and emotional despair I was playing the one string I had left, God was making beautiful music in my life. Something that could have taken my life had turned into a wonderful blessing. In those moments when I felt like there was no hope and reality was slipping from my grasp, I remembered the words God spoke to Paul: "My grace is sufficient for you, for my power is made perfect in weakness" (2 Corinthians 12:9).

My illness had humbled me and made me weak. I was forced into periods of isolation when it was just God and me. During my depression, I tried several medications that did not react well with my body and only made my physical illness worse. Finally, I decided I would do everything humanly possible to work through my depression without medication.

Writing has been a therapeutic way for me to channel negative energy into something fruitful. This method, however, may not work for everyone. For some people battling chronic depression, a medication regimen and consistent therapeutic intervention is best. Whatever method you choose to work through those moments when the only color you see is blue, realize that God is your Shepherd.

Skeptics or faithless people will try to convince you that only a pill, patch, or even an illegal drug can lift the fog of depression that covers your world, yet there are moments—even when you are medicated—when the only comfort you will feel is the presence of the Holy Spirit. Even in the lives of atheists are times when they themselves will have to say, "Oh, my God!" Walking with God does not guarantee your cries will be silenced or your world will be perfect every single day, but His presence makes it easier to push through instead of giving up. On those days when my soul was cast down, I knew the same God who got me through today would get me through tomorrow.

Time has passed and seasons have changed, but I still struggle with my thyroid disease. On some mornings, I wake up feeling exhausted and unable to function normally. During other days, I am riddled with anxiety, mood swings and unable to sift through my thoughts clearly. Over time, I have realized my illness is indeed a thorn in my side that will never be removed. I have also learned not to let things I cannot control consume me, but rather remove myself from stressful situations without reacting inappropriately. I have discovered how to breathe in the fragrance of joy and release the stench of negativity. God's grace and mercy have navigated me through the darkness, and I can honestly say with every fiber of my existence that my hope is built on nothing less than Jesus' blood and righteousness.

When I meditate on the power of hope, I think of the woman with the issue of blood, who is mentioned in several passages of the New Testament. Although the Scriptures tell us that the woman suffered for twelve years with a discharge of blood, just as in the case of Paul's infirmity, they do not reveal what caused this woman's illness. If I relied on a twenty-first century diagnosis and my own personal plight, I would venture to guess that the woman had fibroid tumors, a hormonal abnormality, or an infection that caused chronic bleeding. Whatever the cause of her illness, the weak, pale, physically fragile, and emotionally depleted woman had been ostracized by her community and abandoned by her family. Cloaked in shame, she was considered unclean and was not allowed to be touched.

Tired of living in the margin of life, this woman's hope was built on what she had heard about a man named Jesus. She had not seen Him for herself but merely heard that He was a healer. Determined to be cured from something that doctors could not fix, she headed out to see the man who saves. Desperately making her way through a crowd where she was just another nameless face, she reached out, hoping to touch the man she knew could heal her. Though only able to touch the hem of Jesus' garment, the woman was immediately healed, and the bleeding stopped. Feeling the woman's touch, Jesus immediately asked who touched Him. Then Jesus told the woman her faith had made her well.

When I think of this story and study the different interpretations and translations, I always picture the woman touching the hem of Jesus' garment. I stretch my mind further and see Jesus walking for days on end, traveling near and far, healing and encouraging people. I imagine that as His cloak drags through the dusty roads, His clothes become tattered and His hem frayed. From that frayed hem, a stray string of fabric is sweeping the ground that the woman brushes with her weak and trembling finger. Armed with hope and faith that Jesus can heal her, she reaches out for that one string that holds the miraculous power only Jesus can deliver, and she is made whole.

Perhaps you are like Hope. You appear to be sitting on top of the world, but the reality is you are struggling to hold on and desperately playing the one string you have left. Maybe you thought your life would be filled with a husband, two kids, and a dog, but instead you are single with no prospect in sight. Possibly when you were a child, you dreamed of becoming a dancer. You have been trained and educated at one of the finest performing arts schools in the country. Even though you have put time and energy into developing your talent, rather than performing on stage, you are stuck working in a 4x4 cubicle, wishing you were someplace else.

Maybe your problem is not a family or a dream career. Maybe you are trapped in what appears to be a hopeless emotional state. Depressed, you've alienated yourself from family and friends. You feel alone in a room full of people. Your mind is flooded with thoughts of despair, and you tell yourself that you're worthless and you'll never be happy. Maybe you are emotionally malnourished, unable to forgive people and overcome things that occurred in your past. I'm not sure if any of these scenarios apply to you, but whatever has you sitting on top of the world playing one string, there is hope. Whatever work God has begun in you, He will finish according to His will.

Reflecting on the direction my life was taking in the summer of 2004 prior to moving back to Detroit, I realized that had I not experienced those physical and emotional ordeals, I would not have settled down and written my first novel or even this book. There is indeed a testimony in tragedy. At the time I thought my depression was either a sign of failure or something in me that was broken and could not be fixed. On the contrary, like Paul, through my weakness I accomplished great things that were showered upon me as a gift in the form of grace and mercy. At that moment when you are sitting on top of the world, cast down in blindfolded darkness, reach out and grab that one string and play a tune of hope that reminds you God is always with you.

Reflect on the scriptures below. Under each scripture provide a brief description of what each passage has revealed to you about God's love and protection.

1 I waited patiently for the LORD; he turned to me and heard my cry. 2 He lifted me out of the slimy pit, out of the mud and mire; he set my feet on a rock and gave me a firm place to stand. 3 He put a new song in my mouth, a hymn of praise to our God. Many will see and fear the LORD and put their trust in him. Psalm 40:1-3

8 The LORD himself goes before you and will be with you; he will never leave you nor forsake you. Do not be afraid; do not be discouraged. Deuteronomy 31:8

What areas in your life do you feel are unraveling like a frayed thread? Find a quiet area in your home to pray. Thank God for his love and kindness. Petition God for strength and covering in the midst of your seemingly hopeless situation. Remember, God will never leave you or forsake you.

9
Learning to Limp With Grace

In April of 2007, my pastor preached a sermon on grace that would change my life and help me to heal and repair the broken pieces. The title of the sermon was "Redefined by Grace." The text was taken from 2 Samuel 9:1-7. This sermon talked about how God's grace saves us. After hearing the sermon, I carried its message with me as I began my journey through rediscovery. The following year I officially met Mic Fontaine.

I am so grateful God put me in a place where I was emotionally and spiritually able to open my heart and mind to receive and accept the message that was delivered from both Mic and my pastor. After accepting the fact that I needed to change the way I saw myself, the Spirit moved in such a way it helped me to take those next steps to change. The process was not easy, and downright ugly at times, but through Jesus Christ I am able to say I am happy with myself inside and out. I am happy because God made me, and He DOES NOT make mistakes.

Fall from Grace

Second Samuel 9 takes us on what I like to call a journey of rediscovery, which I began with King David and Mephibosheth. In order for you to understand the significance and the importance of the transformation that took place in Mephibosheth's life, I must first give you some background on him. Mephibosheth was born into royalty as the son of Jonathan and the grandson of King Saul, the first king of Israel. Mephibosheth was born with the name of Mirab Baal, meaning "opponent of Baal," the *false* god. His lineage suggested that because of who his father and grandfather was, he was destined for greatness. After all, he had all the rights and privileges that being the son of a royal father had to offer. His very name suggests that he was intended to be a faithful warrior who would serve and protect.

All of these factors would initially lead us to believe that even as a child, young Mirab Baal was on his way to living the life he was meant to lead. Unfortunately, however, when young Mirab Baal was approximately five years old, his father Jonathan and grandfather King Saul were killed in battle against David and his army. When news spread across the palace that King Saul and Jonathan had been killed, panic filled the palace. People were scrambling to flee for their lives in fear that David would seek revenge on any descendant of King Saul who stood in his way of acquiring the throne.

As the apparent heir to the throne, Mirab Baal was seen as a threat to David, and his life *appeared* to be in danger. In an attempt to protect Mirab Baal from David, his nurse swept him up and ran toward safety. In her haste to get the golden child to safety, the nurse tripped and subsequently dropped Mirab Baal, leaving him lame and crippled, so he was unable to walk and care for himself.

This portion of the biblical story is significant because we are able to identify the precipitating events that led to Mirab Baal's fall from grace. Two significant details stand out regarding how we often handle trouble today. When we are torn from our comfort zone and confronted with what seems like an impossible situation, instead of trusting in God, we panic and make poor choices that alter our lives forever. We also discover that, like young Mirab Baal, our brokenness is caused by an indirect or direct action by someone else, leaving us crippled and lame. At the same time, we fight to rediscover what once made us feel like royalty.

Covered by the Father

Ironically, no one knew that David had no intentions of harming young Mirab Baal. Prior to the events that unfolded, David and Mirab Baal's father Jonathan had been such great friends that they entered into a covenant relationship (1 Samuel 18:20). With his children in mind, Jonathan asked David to promise him he would show kindness to his house forever. This pact meant that David agreed not to harm Jonathan's family, but care for them as he would his own.

In those times, a covenant relationship was a strong bond that could not be broken and must always be honored. It involved a sincere promise of indebtedness that was extended to the heirs of those who entered into the covenant. The people making this pledge basically said to each other, "Whatever I have you have, and whatever you need I will provide. You will not go hungry. I will fight with you and for you, and your family will be taken care of for as long as I live." This is the agreement Jonathan the father formed with David on behalf of his children.

This covenant is like the promise Jesus made on our behalf when He died for our sins. As His children, we are covered by God's grace and mercy. Like young Mirab Baal, when we are vulnerable, we need God the most. When He does not show up when we want Him to, we feel abandoned. But we should never feel lost because when He died on the cross, His blood covered our sins, ensuring that He would always be with us.

Living in Lo Debar

After Mirab Baal was injured, he wore a permanent reminder of his fall from grace. Unable to live with the shame of being crippled, Mirab Baal entered the land of Lo Debar and became known as Mephibosheth, which means "He Who Scatters Shame." Not only would he have to wear a physical reminder of his fall from grace, but now through his name, Mephibosheth would have to wear the badge of shame that had fallen upon him. He would now have to live in a place called Lo Debar, which in some translations means, "Pastureless" and "No Word" in others.

Lo Debar was a place where nothing grew or prospered. When I visualize Lo Debar, I imagine a place with flat lands and miles and miles of dry dirt without vegetation—a place where you could sit and wallow in self-pity for the rest of your life and no one would reach in and pull you out.

With my emotional eye, I picture it as a place that some of us have lived in for what seems like a lifetime. I view Lo Debar as a place where pity and self-doubt festers and causes non-productive complacency. This is the place a descendant of royalty should not be living. As descendants of royalty, we should never live in such a place because Jesus is our portion and He alone is enough to motivate us to live the best life. When reading this passage, I couldn't help but ask this question: are some of us living in Lo Debar because we don't trust God?

Are You Defined by Your Condition?

Years passed, and one day David was in a place of reflection, recalling the blessings God had granted him, when he began to think about his old friend Jonathan. David remembered the promise he made to him years ago to show kindness to his family. David asked, "Is there anyone still left in the house of Saul to whom I can show kindness to for Jonathan's sake?" (2 Samuel 9:1 NIV). David summoned a servant from the household of Saul named Ziba, who informed him that a direct descendant of Jonathan was left—Jonathan's son Mephibosheth.

When Ziba mentions the person who remains from the house of Saul, he does not initially mention him by name, but only by his condition: "There is still a son of Jonathan; he is lame in both feet." (v. 3). We are not given Mephibosheth's name until verse 6 because he is still referenced by his condition and Lo Debar, the barren place where he now lives.

Like Ziba, people often still reference us by our condition instead of our name. We are called the cheater, the liar, the drunk, the drug addict, the crippled, the low-life, etc. In fact, we are even identified by our physical characteristics: the fat one, the skinny one, the one with a limp, the blind one, the deaf one, and the list goes on and on. Sometimes our conditions meet people before we do. We let our conditions define us and determine how we treat others, and most importantly, how we treat ourselves. What do you think God sees when He looks at you? God sees His child whom He loves *unconditionally*. Likewise, we should see each other and ourselves as He sees us.

Is Shame Causing You To Miss Your Blessings?

When King David is informed that a descendant does exist, he isn't concerned about Mephibosheth's physical imperfection, but rather honoring the covenant made between him and Jonathan. David did not hesitate to bless Mephibosheth in spite of his condition. King David sent for Mephibosheth to be brought out of Lo Debar into the palace to receive the blessing his father had secured on his behalf.

Unsettling feelings of fear swept through Mephibosheth's mind as he traveled to meet King David. Ironically, Mephibosheth's fear did not stem from the possibility that King David would have him killed because of his heritage or the people to whom he was related. Instead, his fear derived from a place of insecurity, or low self-esteem.

His feelings emerged because he had lived so long in a place of feeling unworthy due to his physical flaws, and now, he was suddenly ordered to appear in the presence of a king.

As Mephibosheth approached David with his head hung low in shame, teetering from side to side, dragging the lame leg that had been injured when he was crippled long ago, the king saw fear radiating from Mephibosheth, so he told him reassuringly not to be afraid. David explained to Mephibosheth that he was going to show him kindness for the sake of his father Jonathan by restoring to him all the land that belonged to his grandfather Saul. David placed his hand on Mephibosheth's shoulder, looked deep into his eyes, and assured him that he would always eat at the king's table. Shocked and still wearing the shame of his deformity, Mephibosheth bowed down before the king with his head hanging low and carrying the weight of his brokenness. Trembling, he said, "What is your servant, that you should notice a dead dog like me?" (v. 8).

This was the turning point in Mephibosheth's life. At that moment his condition, label, or badge of shame did not matter because he was covered by a promise made by his father. I imagine Mephibosheth finally saw beyond the low self-esteem and what others thought of him by realizing he was a descendant of a king. In my mind, Mephibosheth rediscovered that five-year-old boy who was lost, and reclaimed the blessings he'd been promised at birth.

Many of us are like Mephibosheth. As a result of events that crippled us long ago, we are still suffering from low self-esteem and a sense of diminished self-worth. We just can't get past the badge of shame or the label of affliction we've been wearing for years. Our minds are so cluttered with negative thoughts that we say "no" before we say "yes." We don't even realize that we have conditioned ourselves to think we are born to fail and cannot move forward.

The NIV translation uses the word "notice" in verse 8. Mephibosheth could not believe the king noticed *"someone like him."* Mephibosheth walked with his head down for so long, trying to go unnoticed, that he never looked up to "notice" someone wanted to bless him.

This awesome story reminds me of my experience a few years ago when I was dating a gentleman who gave me compliments constantly and called me beautiful more times than I could count. He was always lifting me up and trying to make me feel like I was beautiful and worthy. Unfortunately, because the veil of low self-esteem was blinding my eyes, I could not accept the love he was trying to give. One day I mentioned to him that I thought he wanted someone who had a better shape than I. He said something to me that would stick with me forever. He said, "That's your insecurity, not mine. To me, you're beautiful."

When I was ten years old, I learned to hate my body and my looks. I never thought I was pretty because people always made me feel there was something wrong with the way I looked. But even before that humiliating incident on the playground, I had been dropped by someone else, so I suffered through years of shame that would hinder me from being who I truly was, the authentic person God intended me to be. For most of my life, I had lived in a place where I could not accept compliments because I felt I wasn't worthy. Instead, all that time I defined my worth as a person by some physical attribute.

When I reached adulthood, I was given several opportunities to live my life in front of a camera as a news anchor. Since I was a child, I had always wanted to be a news anchor, but I never saw in myself what others saw, so I was afraid to follow my dreams and accept the blessings God was trying to give. As time passed and I continued to live in Lo Debar, I prayed faithfully that God would deliver me from that barren land. When I wrote my first book, I was given another chance to follow a dream, so I packed my bags and moved from Lo Debar into the land of emotional and spiritual prosperity and freedom.

At that time, I realized that due to our new birth in Christ, we have entered into a covenant with God that says no matter what we've done, we are covered and will always eat from the King's table in spite of ourselves. Believing in Him means believing in ourselves. God takes us as weak and lame, just as we are, and covers us with His grace and mercy. We are all born with an inherent gift from God that makes us special. Sometimes we are thrown off track, crippled, or broken by some event that happens to change our course, but we are never lost with God as our guide. Through God's awesome grace and mercy, despite our condition, we will always eat at His table. God did not create us to walk around with our head hung low, seeing ourselves as dead dogs. Even if life has dealt us a blow that causes us to walk with a limp, we should limp as a child of the King would—with God's wonderful grace.

10
Unapologetically Authentically Bourgeois

When I was younger, I had big plans for my life: I was going to begin my career as a television news reporter and ultimately become the next Oprah Winfrey. After retiring from a career in television, I would spend my golden years teaching African-American studies as an adjunct professor at a college or university somewhere in the South. I would live on a ranch, raise cattle, and ride horses all day. At night I'd sit on my wraparound porch sipping sweet tea with my two Rottweilers, Jack and Molly. If marriage was meant for me, I would welcome it with open arms, but if not, I'd still be just fine sitting on my porch with my three golden girls: my grandmother, mother, and aunt Thell.

While attending Tougaloo College, I began my career in radio. I was a part-time radio announcer named Kandi. In my own mind, at the age of nineteen everything was set and falling into place. When I graduated from college and moved to Houston, however, my plans changed. The radio and television industry was all about who you know, not what you know. I couldn't even get an internship at a television or radio station. The only job that I could find was subbing at an elementary school. As the end of the year approached and we prepared for the Christmas holiday break, I lay my head on my desk and prayed that God would deliver me from teaching. I'd spent the semester subbing for a teacher who was out on maternity leave. One thing I knew at the end of the semester was that teaching kindergarten was not my gift. So, I gave up.

At the advice of a friend, I applied for a position with Children's Protective Services (CPS). A few days before returning to school after the Christmas holiday, I was offered a job at CPS. I felt like I had been delivered from whining five-year-olds with sticky hands pulling on me all day demanding my attention. Boy, was I in for a surprise! I had just jumped out of the frying pan into open flames. I spent the next eleven years in the Health and Human Services field. During my tenure, I thought it was the worst experience of life. I just knew that I was being punished for something. So, I gave up.

In 2004 I wrote my first book, *The Green Eyed Butterfly* and followed up with two more books in 2005. I felt confident that I was destined to be a great writer climbing up the best seller lists. Still holding on to my ambition to be in radio and television, I wanted to do it all. There was no reason why I couldn't do everything that I wanted to do. I thought I'd write a book, print it, and people would buy it and I'd be a millionaire. The problem was that I failed to plan. My first five hundred copies were a nightmare because the manuscript contained numerous errors and included a duplicate chapter. I ended up giving away over half of my inventory. I spent thousands of dollars traveling to book fairs but hardly sold any books. I sent out books for review, yet years later, I'm still waiting to hear something. Money spent on advertising was like throwing money out of an open window into the abyss.

Despite my failure to properly plan, *The Green Eyed Butterfly* was well received by readers. People reported staying home from work or staying up all night to finish reading this book. I am grateful to those who supported me and continue to encourage me to write. Unfortunately, the support and reviews weren't enough to drown out the no that I heard from other people. Instead of enjoying a small victory, I was waiting on something grand like being on the *New York Times* best seller's list. So, I gave up.

Don't Let Go, Just Say Yes

After throwing in the towel on my hopes and dreams, I grew weary and wondered what I was doing wrong. One day while sitting in my back yard, I asked God what He wanted from me. I knew that I had talent. I knew that deep down I wasn't a quitter, but professionally nothing ever felt completely comfortable to me. I felt disconnected, experiencing fleeting moments of success, yet still wanting something even grander. I wanted something that would make me feel like I had truly accomplished something. I wanted something that would allow me to stick my chest out and say, "Look what I did."

I had the audacity to ask God why He gave me the gift to write yet not bless me with the sale of hundreds of thousands of copies so I could collect a fat check. I knew that God had given me His yes to write, but I couldn't figure out why I would sit in front of my computer all day and night and pour myself into my writing, only to gain a few bucks. So, I figured it must not be in God's plan for me to be a successful writer. I continued to write fiction for my own personal enjoyment. After I completed a book, I would bind it and store it in the back of my closet.

Frustrated and unmotivated, I began to take an account of my life and review all the things I'd done professionally. I failed to mention that ever since I was a teenager, God has been telling me that He had a plan for me and I needed to trust Him, yet I wanted no part of His plan. Throughout my professional career, God continually called me closer to Him, but I would ignore His call and move on to what I wanted. God had been calling me to a life in ministry, but I kept asking the wrong questions. I asked God over and over again, "Do You know who You're talking to?" *Why in the world would God call me to ministry? If I thought dating was a challenge before this, now who would date me? Would I have to stop drinking my favorite Cognac? Would I have to stop writing adult fiction? Does He know how messed up I am right now?* All of my questions were about me and what I wanted.

Hundreds of questions kept swimming around in my head. Instead of waiting for God to answer my questions, I answered them myself and continued to say no to His command. Finally, one day I was at work sitting at my desk when I felt the overwhelming presence of God rush over me. I felt like a cup that was running over at a rapid rate and nothing was there to catch the overflow. I began to cry and lost control of my emotions. God was showing me what He wanted from me, but I was so afraid that I shut my eyes and started shaking my head. I tried to shake what I was seeing out of my head. I slid my chair away from my desk and got up to walk around the building to collect my thoughts. I just knew that after all those other failed attempts at losing my mind, it was finally happening. I was convinced that the final screw had come loose in my head and I was on my way to the psych ward.

After convincing myself that I was indeed "loosing it," I laughed at myself and went back to my office. Still feeling both fragile and full, I sat down at my desk trying to think about anything other than what was brewing inside me. I could not rest, however, so I shut my computer down, grabbed my purse, my cellphone, and car keys, and headed home. I cried all the way home. This wasn't a cute little cry that made me dab the corners of my eyes with Kleenex tissue; instead, this was a big, ugly, snotty cry that blinded my eyesight. I pulled into the garage, opened the door, and ran up the stairs to my bedroom. I walked around, praying and crying until I felt like I was going to suffocate. I argued with God, presenting all the reasons why I would not follow His command.

My battle lasted for hours. Light turned into dark, and finally I was exhausted beyond measure. My energy was gone. My tear ducts were dry, and my eyes began to get heavy. My nose was so congested, I could hardly breathe. I felt disoriented and my body became heavy, like I had been in a fight with a sumo wrestler. I felt like Jacob, who wrestled with God all night long until He blessed him. I refused to let go, not giving up until I knew for sure what God wanted from me.

Finally, I stopped in my tracks and walked toward the hallway, where I lay down with my face pressed against the cold, hard floor. Everything around me was silent, and I could not hear a sound. There was no outside noise—no television, no phone ringing, just silence. Finally, I asked, "Lord, please tell me what You want from me?" I told God that I wasn't moving from that spot until we came to a mutual understanding. The funny thing is that I was the only one with a bad understanding of what was happening to me.

Lying on the floor in a fetal position, I heard two words, "submit" and "obedient." I realized then that if I did that, I would have more than I ever asked for. God wanted to give me rest and a sound mind, but I could not have those things as long as I was disobedient. God revealed that He was going to empty me so that He could fill me up to pour into others.

Exhausted, I raised myself up from the floor and sat with my back pressed against the wall. I threw my hands up in the air and said, "I'm Yours, Lord." I said, "Okay, Lord, it's just me and You. I am Yours." I could not fight anymore, so this time I did not give up—I simply submitted.

I didn't even have to ask as God began speaking to me about the path that He'd prepared for me. Everything that I'd been through—the rejection, broken relationships, abandonment, unforgiveness, abuse, and redirected career paths—were all part of His plan. As hard as it all may have seemed at the time, coming to Houston with one suitcase, no car, no job, no real plan and benefiting from the kindness of a friend's spare room was no accident. Working with CPS and in the behavioral health field was no accident. Working at the church was no accident. Writing my first two books had not been in vain. God wasn't saying no to a successful career as an author; instead, He was saying not yet.

Everything that I had done up until the moment I was sitting in a dark hallway at 2:00 a.m. had prepared me for God's plan for my life. I am here as a living witness to tell you that everything you are going through in life—the good, the bad, and the ugly—is meant to build you, not to break you. I've discovered that sometimes you have to have a break down in order to have a breakthrough.

Although I said yes and my burden began to feel lighter, I was still worried, primarily about how people would react to my call. Unfortunately, there is still a stigma that brands women in ministry. What would people think of me? Would my family and friends support me? Unfortunately, not everyone in my life supports me, not even those closest to me. I currently attend Truett Theological Seminary at Baylor University. My commute is a five-hour round trip from Houston to Waco every Monday. At the same time, I am working a full-time job at a "mega church" and managing a physically and emotionally life-altering thyroid disease. To top it off, I began my first semester at Truett battling a pituitary gland issue that affected my cognitive functioning. Indeed, there was a 360-degree attack being waged on my physical and emotional health.

There were several people who didn't understand my journey, believing that I was foolish for making the weekly trip. Behind my back, some people felt the need to discuss whether or not I was following God's plan. Some were even bold enough to encourage me to consider revising my plan and quit school. My actions may not have made sense to them, but it made sense to God and me. Thankfully, there were others who supported me with words of encouragement every step of the way. When I became weary and considered leaving Truett, God said that He didn't call the nay-sayers; He called me.

Authentically Bourgeois

The simple truth is that most of us spend a lifetime searching for something that lives deep inside, waiting to be discovered. Instead of embracing who we are at our core, we wear masks that hide our authentic selves. These masks conceal our truth and become a method of survival. It is easier to wear a mask rather than risk revealing our weaknesses, leaving us open for attack or rejection because we do not think or act the way normal society says we should. These masks hide our insecurities, flaws, and vulnerabilities. Wearing a mask robs us of our individual uniqueness.

For years I wore a mask shielding me and the rest of the world from who I really was at my core. I'd always known that I was different, but I always wanted to fit in somewhere and belong to something. I never understood that God did not design me to follow but to lead. (There are those people in your life—some strangers and others disguised as well-meaning friends—who will try to convince you that you are not capable or worthy of greatness.)

When I was growing up in my church in Detroit, there was a young lady in the youth choir who always had a nasty attitude. At the time, she was in high school and a couple of years older than I. Even at a young age she always seemed miserable and complained about everything. She even talked with this slow and unconcerned twang. When she spoke, she always tilted her head to the side as if she could not hold her head up to look people in the eye. She would always pick on me, and I never had any idea why. One day during choir rehearsal, she just flat out told me she didn't like me. She said I was "Bougee" and fake. She said I thought I was cute.

Hearing the girl say she did not like me hurt me to my core. I had no idea why she didn't like me. I could not understand how at twelve years old, someone could be Bougee or fake. *What did or does being Bougee and fake really mean?* I wondered. I was only being myself. For years after that moment, I could still hear and feel her spitting those words at me like stones. As time passed, I heard the word "Bougee" over and over again in different settings or situations, but the intent was the same. I would not only hear the word to describe myself, but other women who appeared to be smart, ambitious, and attractive. After hearing this time and time again, I began to think there was something wrong with being just who I was.

Just in case you've never heard the word "Bougee" or can't imagine how the word is meant as an insult, I'll give you a lesson in Urban Vernacular 101. "Bourgeois" or "bou-gee" (boo`-zhie), as it is pronounced in the urban vernacular (slang), is a term used to describe arrogant, upscale, or snobbish characteristics. This is a term typically used as a derogatory statement suggesting you are "uppity" or trying to be in a higher social status than you deserve. During my youth, people often referred to me as being "Bougee" because of my outward appearance and mannerisms. The truth is that I was far from "Bougee." I was battling low self-esteem, along with a poor perception of what I thought I looked like.

Over time I realized the young lady did not have a problem with me, but with who she was at that point in her own life. She needed to make someone else miserable, and during Thursday night choir rehearsal she designated me as her target for an hour and half each week. I am an adult now and the word "Bourgeois" or "Bougee" still exists, but my feelings about the words have changed. I resolved that if being Bourgeois means I am confident, intelligent, God-fearing, educated, strong, sexy, and an extraordinary woman, then I guess I am unapologetically authentically Bourgeois.

The way we treat others is a clear indication of how we feel about ourselves. The way we see ourselves is vital to how we live our lives each day. Relationships also play a major role in our lives. How we interact with others, who we choose as friends, who we date, and how we allow others to treat us are key indications of how we feel about ourselves. Our relationships and how we conduct ourselves in them reveal our insecurities.

Relationships with others are important, but the most important earthly relationship is the one that you have with yourself. If you don't love yourself, it makes it difficult for others to love you. Loving yourself means loving who you are and accepting that God loves you in spite of the labels you have placed on yourself and those others have placed on you. Loving yourself means loving who you are in spite of your circumstance, infirmity, or sin. Perhaps your inability to live an authentic life is due to your poor self-image and inability to maintain a healthy loving relationship with yourself.

You cannot change the way you see yourself until you are honest about who you are authentically at your core—not how others see you, but how you feel when no one else is looking. Knowing who you truly are will help you become the person God has designed you to be. Our self-image is the picture etched in our minds and carried in our souls. Our self-image is what we see each time we look in the mirror. If what we see are unhealthy, insecure pictures of fear, doubt, shame, and hopelessness, then we have already dishonored God's creation. Genesis 1:27 (NIV) says, "So God created mankind in his own image, in the image of God he created them; male and female he created them."

I remember the pain of living an unauthentic life. I felt like there was a constant weight sitting on my chest that would not allow the real me to get out and shine. It was an uncomfortable and unhappy place that kept me from living my best life. I was caught up in being the person I thought others wanted me to be or who I should be in that particular environment. I had strayed away from the person I knew God created me to be. I started going along to get along by dumbing myself down to make others feel more important than they truly were. I started to question my talents, my intellect, and my ability to do something I was born to do. I did not care about my appearance and no longer felt sexy. I'd totally lost myself.

It was an agonizing space to live in, until one day I looked around and had no idea who I really was. I started to ask myself, *Am I living authentically? Who am I at my core? Am I living my life as one of the fictitious characters I write about in my novels? Am I living the life God designed for me?* Just as God does time and time again, He showed up right on time—when I was at my breaking point. My friend Mic told me that he wanted that confident, secure and ambitious woman he met years ago to show up. I'd lost that thing that made me unique, confident, and carefree.

This conversation was God-sent. I felt like the blinders had been ripped off my eyes, and now I needed to dig deep inside and sift through the rubble of my life, clean out the trash, and recycle that trash into something useful. I needed to clear an unobstructed pathway that would allow me to see who I was authentically.

Living authentically is about knowing who you are at your core, accepting the real you, and understanding it's really not about you and definitely not about those whose mission is to make you feel like who you are is not good enough. Living authentically means you understand that it is about God's purpose for your life and what you can do to positively impact the lives of others.

What it Means to be Authentically Bourgeois

Bourgeois (boor ZHwä) Bou-gie(noun)(verb) a woman who is bold enough to be who she is authentically. She accepts nothing less than extraordinary. She may bend, but not break. Can't is not in her vocabulary. Her faith is unyielding. Her beauty radiates from within. She is confident, she is amazing, she is sexy, she is powerful...she is unapologetically Bourgeois.

Who Am I Authentically?

I have often been described as quirky and random. In fact, some people have a hard time figuring me out. One friend refers to me as consistently inconsistent and unpredictable. The truth is that I am all of those things they've described. If I were a vegetable or a spice, I would be an onion because I have many layers yet to be explored. I credit my personality to my upbringing and environmental exposure.

In the summer of 1994, I moved to Detroit to live with my mother. The move was a total culture shock. I'd gone from a small town in Mississippi where everyone knew me and I felt comfortable and safe to a huge city where no one knew my name and no one really cared who I was or wasn't.

My quiet, uneventful life had been turned upside down. I went from feeling safe to always being on guard and ready for a fight at any moment. Girls in Detroit did not carry lip-gloss in their purses; instead, they carried box cutters. After realizing that I would remain a resident of Detroit until I graduated from high school, I decided that either I had to adapt to my environment and act accordingly or be devoured and digested into the belly of the big city. Things that would shock the sheltered little Southern belle from Mississippi became a normal, everyday occurrence for the resilient little girl from southwest Detroit.

From fourth to twelfth grade, I felt like I was walking on a balance beam trying to manage two different personalities. During the school year, my environment consisted of sneaking to parties that ended in shots fired, leaving us ducking under tables for safety. Role models were the local dope dealers. We were fascinated by the boys in the neighborhood who were "rollin'." Even at a young age, jail and death was an ever-present reality for my classmates.

Fortunately, when I entered the eighth grade, my mother had the forethought to enroll me in private school, but the influence was never too far away. There are two significant events that occurred in my adolescent years that helped to shape the way that I approached adulthood. One morning when I was in junior high, I awoke to the news that two of my classmates had been found dead under the bridge at the end of my uncle's street. Both boys had been executed. After the bodies were removed from under the bridge, we mourned the loss and talked about it among ourselves in the neighborhood, but life went on as normal.

The second incident occurred at the age of sixteen. While riding down a street where my friends and I were forbidden to go, I saw a boy I knew get shot in the head and fall over dead just a few feet away from us. After seeing the boy's body hit the ground, the light turned green and we rolled through in silence. We mourned the loss and talked about it among ourselves in the neighborhood, but life went on as normal. Throughout elementary school, junior high, and high school, friends were shot, stabbed, killed, and incarcerated as they battled addiction and sold drugs. We mourned the loss and talked about it among ourselves in the neighborhood, but life went on as normal. It was just a part of growing up. Sometimes, I think about those boys that were killed and wonder who they could have been as men. I realize that we have to appreciate the time that God gives us on earth and use it wisely.

At the end of every school year, I would return to my quiet, unassuming town and reprogram myself to relax and enjoy the peaceful summer. When I went off to college and people asked where I was from, depending on my mood, I'd say Mississippi or Detroit. For years I hated the fact that I lived in Detroit. I blamed every negative thing that happened from age six to eighteen on my connection to Detroit. For me, moving to Detroit symbolized an inner struggle to figure out where I really fit in. On one hand, my Mississippi friends could not relate to my Detroit experience, and my Detroit friends could not relate to Mississippi experience on the other hand.

I have always felt like two people living in one body fighting over which Kiffany would show up on any given day. Finally I realized that I would not be who I am without all I've experienced, the places I've lived, and the things I've seen throughout my life. Fortunately, growing up in Mississippi and Detroit has molded me into a well-rounded woman. There are some Detroit influences that have made me strong, street-smart, and capable of handling myself in any environment and still be *Bougee*. There are some Mississippi influences that have fostered within me a sensibility of compassion, strong roots, and Southern charm. We have all been in positions that seemed

Who Am I Authentically?

unbearably uncomfortable at the time, but each circumstance has in some way made us more resilient.

After graduating from high school, I lost touch with friends whom I had known since my elementary school days. Fortunately, through the power of social media, I have been able to reconnect and celebrate their lives, families, friendships, and accomplishments. When I see photos of them hanging out together as adults, I miss them dearly and only think about the good times.

Authentically, I am a girl from southwest Detroit by way of Batesville, Mississippi. According to the Myers-Briggs Personality Test, my personality type is INFP (Introverted Feeling with Extraverted Intuition). My favorite place in the world is sitting in my back yard with my laptop typing out a new story. I am impatient yet attentive to the needs of others. In order to protect my own peace, I avoid drama and chaos. To some I am quiet and reserved. To others I am a spontaneous comedian who might start singing the theme to the "Love Boat" at any given moment.

I am a fan of old-school hip-hop, some mornings I have to listen to a little 8 Ball and MJG just to get my day started. I believe Tupac is alive and living in the Caribbean; he is my Elvis. I love Andrea Bocelli and my favorite song in the whole world is Reba McEntire's "Fancy." My dream vehicle is not a Bentley or Lamborghini, it is a four-door black Jeep Wrangler. I find more enjoyment sitting outside enjoying the peace of a spring breeze than partying like a rock star all night. People often accuse me of being antisocial, but the truth is that God has blessed me with a discerning spirit and I can sense when someone is not genuine. Since I believe that authentic connections flow naturally, I don't force relationships of any kind. I can't stand foolishness. My facial expressions don't lie; typically, I cannot hide my true feelings. I have a very strong personality, I am very outspoken, and I have to think before I speak most of the time.

Honestly, I am not for everyone and I am okay with that. Not everyone will love or like me, and I'm okay with that. Not everyone will support me or understand where God is leading me, and I'm okay with that. Some people will look at me and say, "Who is she to encourage or motivate me?" and I'm okay with that. The fact is that God chose me in spite of how others feel about me or even how I feel about myself.

During my journey of writing this book, I was afraid of what people would say. *How would people react to my truth?* I often wondered. I sat on the *Change the Way You See Yourself* book for quite a while because I was afraid, but God revealed to me that was selfish. I was selfishly holding on to something that would bless someone else. Through my own journey to empty my emotional trash can, I have learned not to question God and ask Him why certain situations have occurred in my life. Now I thank God for trusting me with tragedy and deferred dreams.

So, who am I authentically? Authentically, I am a woman whose passion and purpose is to help you empty your emotional trash can, to clear away the rubbish that keeps you from seeing yourself as God sees you.

www.ingramcontent.com/pod-product-compliance
Lightning Source LLC
Chambersburg PA
CBHW072101290426
44110CB00014B/1773